EASTER AND
HYBRID LILY
PRODUCTION

GROWERS HANDBOOK SERIES
VOLUME 5

Allan M. Armitage, General Editor

EASTER AND HYBRID LILY PRODUCTION

Principles and Practice

William B. Miller

Department of Horticulture
Clemson University
Clemson, SC 29634 U.S.A.

TIMBER PRESS
Portland, Oregon

Cover illustrations
Front: Greenhouse full of budded Easter lilies.

Back:
Figures 27a–c. New Oriental hybrid lilies with
rapid forcing times and pot culture adaptability.

ISBN 0-88192-205-6
Printed in Hong Kong

TIMBER PRESS, INC.
9999 S.W. Wilshire, Suite 124
Portland, Oregon 97225

Library of Congress Cataloging-in-Publication Data

Miller, William Blanchard, 1959–
    Easter and hybrid lily production : principles and practice /
William B. Miller.
        p.   cm. -- (Growers handbook series ; v. 5)
    Includes bibliographical references and index.
    ISBN 0-88192-205-6
    1. Lilies. 2. Easter lily.   I. Title. II. Series.
SB413.L7M56   1992
635.9'34324--dc20
                                                        91-19986
                                                        CIP

Contents

Acknowledgments

I am grateful to Allan Armitage for his invitation to write this book, and for his editorial patience. Also, I express thanks to Dr. Robert O. Miller, Dahlstrom and Watt Bulb Farms, Inc., Smith River, Calif., for reviewing the entire manuscript; and to Mr. John Vandenberg, Vandenberg Bulb Co., Chester, N.Y., for reviewing the section on Asiatic hybrids. Acknowledgment is also extended to the many researchers whose published and unpublished findings are presented within.

Introduction

In this book, cultural and production information about Easter and hybrid lilies has been collected. Although volumes of literature have been published on the growth, development, and cultural aspects of Easter lilies, much less information is available concerning greenhouse forcing of asiatic lilies, and even less about oriental hybrids. However, many principles are the same for these different lilies, and generalizations may certainly be made. In some cases—such as the response to cooling, fertilization, and post-production storage—the groups behave differently. The similarities and differences in production techniques for various lily species will be stressed when appropriate.

In the United States in 1989 and 1990, potted Easter lilies had a wholesale value of $33.1 and $36.9 million, respectively (data from the 28 states with the largest production). The 28 states that reported data had over 1400 growers, a production area of 7.1 million square feet, and produced over 9.5 million pots (Agricultural Statistics Board, U.S., 1991). Based on production square footage, the data suggest about 11.6 million pots grown. Canadian production has been estimated to be over 1 million pots, and is not included in U.S. production statistics. If such trends continued into the 1990s, the value of the Easter lily crop will soon be well over $50 million. Clearly, lilies are an important crop, and presently are fourth in wholesale value in the United States pot plant market, behind poinsettia ($183 million), chrysanthemum ($96 million), and azalea ($55 million) (Agricultural Statistics Board, U.S., 1991).

It is often said, however, that potted lilies can be the most profitable floricultural crop grown. Easter lilies can also be one of the most difficult. I hope this book will help to increase the understanding of this exciting crop.

Lily Biology

Native Environment

The Easter lily (*Lilium longiflorum* Thunb.) was first botanically described by Carl Peter Thunberg in 1794. It is native to the tropical Liukiu Archipelago, which includes the islands Okinawa and Oshima, and the Kawanabe island chain. Wilson (1925) found the plant growing in "pockets in the coral rock by the sea. It appears to be a maritime plant, and, unlike most lilies, a limestone plant."

One legend has it that the Easter lily arrived in Bermuda after a storm damaged a ship traveling from the Orient to England. The crippled ship landed in Bermuda, and a missionary on board left some bulbs he had collected in Taiwan with the island's rector as repayment for hospitality during the ship's repairs. Later, after the plants were flourishing on Bermuda, a Philadelphia florist brought bulbs back to grow in his greenhouse, thus introducing Easter lilies to the United States.

Morphology

BULB MORPHOLOGY

The Easter lily bulb is a compressed shoot consisting of a basal plate (stem) and numerous fleshy, nontunicate scales (Fig. 1). Because of the absence of a papery protective tunic (such as that on garlic cloves or hyacinth

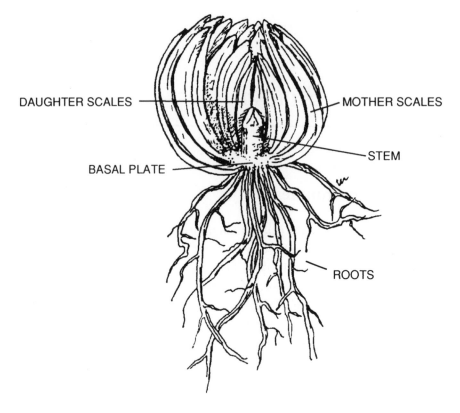

Figure 1. Morphology of the Easter lily bulb.

bulbs), Easter lily bulbs must always be held in moist peat moss or other material to minimize water loss during storage and shipping. The scales, which are actually modified leaves, contain carbohydrate reserves used when the bulb is forced in the greenhouse (Miller and Langhans 1989a, 1989b). During forcing, bulbs change from producing scale-leaves to producing green, photosynthetic leaves. These rhythmic changes are complex, and are governed by several environmental conditions, including temperature, day length, and cultural conditions during bulb production (Roberts et al. 1985).

PLANT MORPHOLOGY

At flowering, the above-ground parts consist of a stem, leaves, and flowers. Below-ground features are stem and basal roots, bulb remnants (with the outer scales almost entirely depleted), inner scales, and a new, developing bulblet in the center of the bulb (Fig. 2).

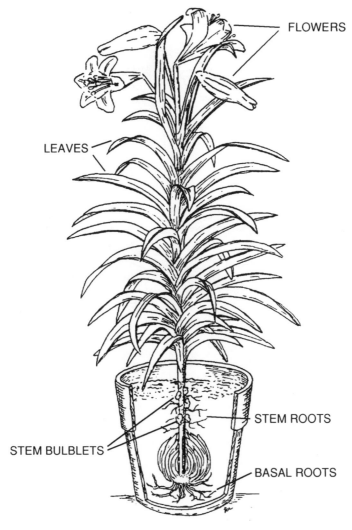

Figure 2. Morphology of the Easter lily plant.

7

FLOWER MORPHOLOGY

In most lily flowers, the petals and sepals are nearly identical, and are referred to as tepals. The flower consists of six stamens (composed of an anther and filament) and one pistil (with a stigma, style, and ovary) (Fig. 3).

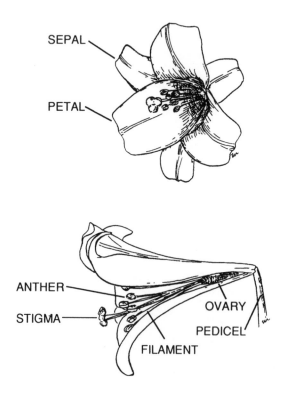

Figure 3. Morphology of the Easter lily flower.

West Coast Bulb Production

History

Green (1986) recently reported that the vast majority of Easter lily bulb production in the United States and Canada occurs in the northern California/southern Oregon coastal strip. This narrow area has a Mediterranean climate with cool, dry summers and mild, wet winters. The soils are rich in organic matter and are well-drained, a necessity in an area receiving 70–120 in. of annual rainfall. Griffiths (1930) enumerated numerous environmental characteristics necessary for bulb production such as relatively low yearly average temperatures, high relative humidity, abundant rainfall, and rich, well drained soils high in organic matter. These characteristics are all found along this coastal strip, making it particularly well suited for lily bulb production. Limited bulb production continues in the southern United States, with most bulbs being used for cut flowers (Wilkins 1980).

In 1908, Bermuda was the main source of Easter lily bulbs in the United States (Oliver 1908), but the bulbs were of low quality due to high levels of virus diseases, and 50–75% of the bulbs were unusable. Prior to 1908, experimental plots in Florida (Miami and Key West), California (San Francisco, Santa Ana, Ventura, and Long Beach), Arizona (Yuma), and Texas (Brownsville) yielded favorable results for bulb production, but, for various reasons, a bulb production industry never developed at any of these locations (Oliver 1908). Japan was a major source of lily bulbs in the 1920s to late 1930s.

The Pacific Northwestern bulb production industry began in earnest at the outbreak of World War II, when importation of Japanese bulbs was halted. At its zenith, over 400 growers were producing crops in small backyard plots in the area of Brookings, Oregon, and Smith River, California. Currently, there are fewer than 10 growers in the region, producing over 10 million bulbs each year, accounting for nearly all of the Easter lily bulb production in the United States and Canada. Asiatic and Oriental hybrid lilies are produced in this same area and into upper Washington state. Accurate production statistics for hybrid bulbs are not available.

Modern Bulb Production

The descriptions below relate primarily to Easter lilies. Three years of field growth are necessary to produce a "commercial" (6.5–10 in. circumference) bulb, if scale propagation is employed. Each year, the bulbs are dug, sorted for size, then replanted. Bulb production is very labor-intensive, but equipment for mechanization is constantly being upgraded, almost exclusively from Dutch sources.

During the first year in the field, the scale initiates an adventitious bulb, and grows. When dug the following fall, the new bulb is 2.5–5 in. in circumference. When replanted, it is referred to as a "scalet," and continues to grow for another season. When dug at the end of the second year, the propagule is referred to as a "yearling." At the end of the third year, the bulb is of greenhouse forcing size, and called "commercial" (Fig. 4). One year is removed from this scheme if the grower starts with vigorous (3–4 in. circumference) stem bulblets.

In the case of hybrid lilies, bulbs are sold by metric circumference, with 10–12 cm (and larger) being the commonly forced sizes. Production of commercial bulbs usually requires only one year from the scalet phase (two years total).

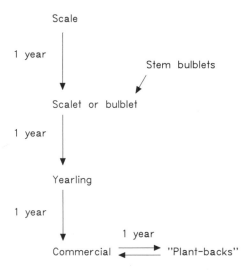

Figure 4. Field production scheme for Easter lily bulbs in the Pacific Northwest.

Propagation

Several methods of propagating lilies are used commercially. The most common means are vegetative methods, and their principal advantage is clone establishment. Seed propagation, while not used for commercial bulb production, is important in breeding and new cultivar development.

SCALING

The major method of vegetative propagation is by fleshy scales. In commercial practice, commercial (saleable) bulbs are lifted from fields in the late summer or early fall, and brought to the processing shed where scales are removed. Scales are washed on a conveyor chain, treated with liquid fungicide, and returned to a new field for planting. They are distributed in rows, and are planted at a density of about 35 to 50 scales per linear foot. Planting rows are about 12–14 in. wide. Exogenous hormone (auxin) application is not beneficial in increasing yield or size of scalets. Adventitious buds soon form during the winter season, and develop into small bulbs or "scalets." The scalets sprout in the spring and form small plants. Some, perhaps 20%, of these plants will form one or two flowers during the first summer. In the field, some scales die because of disease or pest attack, and other scales are too small to produce a vigorous new plant. Because of this loss, each scale yields about 0.5 usable scalet, or about 15 to 25 scalets per linear foot.

The adventitious scalets almost always arise on the basal portion of the scale, and generally are associated with a wounded surface. Some bulb growers heat treat scales (111°F for 1 hr.) prior to planting to eliminate a foliar nematode prior to replanting.

In the case of valuable new cultivars, a modification of this method may be employed, where scales are placed in moist vermiculite and wrapped in polyethylene. They are held at 70° to 72°F for several weeks to several months, resulting in a larger crop of scalets in a shorter time. Additionally, after the first crop of scalets are removed from the scale, healthy scales may be replanted in fresh vermiculite, and a partial second crop may result, depending on the cultivar. In both cases, resulting scalets (with scales attached if possible) are planted into fields in the fall.

STEM BULBLETS

Depending on cultivar, many stem bulblets may form and develop after flowering. Stem bulblets are expanded buds from axils of underground leaf nodes. The stem bulblets are complete and consist of roots, scales, basal plate, and meristem. Bulbs are dug, and the detached stem bulblets are replanted in the field in August or September. The principal advantage of using stem bulblets (relative to scaling) is the savings of a full year of production time. The labor and volume of material that must be handled, however, are substantially greater than for scaling. Again, as this is a vegetative procedure, the clone is maintained.

AERIAL STEM BULBILS

Many species of *Lilium* produce structures which are outgrowths of the axillary buds associated with the leaves of the upright shoot. These are aerial bulbils and are usually dark in color, and are comprised of several shortened scales and a meristem. Roots are usually not seen on stem bulbils. These structures may be removed and placed in a moist substrate. Roots form, followed by leaf and shoot development. Usually, two to three years of growth is necessary for flowering to occur depending on species and cultivar. Easter lilies do not normally form stem bulbils, but many cultivars of the Asiatic and Oriental hybrid groups readily form these aerial structures.

LEAF CUTTINGS

Detached Easter lily leaves will form bulblets at the leaf base when propagated, similar to many other species. Detached leaves, buried 1.5 cm in moist vermiculite at 70°F, form an average of about two bulblets per leaf. Leaves from the upper portion of the plant provide the best success (80% regeneration), and basal leaves the poorest (40%). This method has also been reported to work with 'Enchantment' and *L. lancifolium* (Roh 1982).

13

TISSUE CULTURE

This method is used mainly for the rapid increase of a new cultivar prior to field growth. Lilies are easy to establish in tissue culture, with generally favorable propagation rates. Although tissue culture laboratories are difficult to set up and maintain, several commercial laboratories are available to contract out the propagation of a new cultivar. The main advantage of contracting is that individual growers do not have to invest in expensive capital equipment, but simply pay the lab for each plant delivered.

Agar culture is the basic method in lily tissue culture propagation. Typically, MS salts and several vitamins compose the basal nutrient medium. Auxin, usually naphthalene acetic acid (NAA), is used to promote scalet formation (Stimart and Ascher 1978). Scales are surface sterilized for 20 min. in 10% clorox solution, with a detergent. After rinsing with sterile water, scales are sectioned and placed onto the medium. New structures invariably arise on the basal portion of the scale, and also on the inner side of the scale. After a period of growth, the new plantlets may be hardened off, grown in the greenhouse in the summer, then transplanted to the field in the fall.

Field Preparation and Outdoor Operations

For field production, field preparation begins in early June. Currently, most growers use a crop rotation of one year in lilies, and two to four years in pasture and forage. The cover crop is pulverized, usually by rototiller or several passes with a disk, followed by perpendicular passes with a sub-soiling implement. This tool breaks up the plow pan, and works at a depth of 15–22 in. Fields are plowed to a depth of 10–14 in. After plowing, several passes with a disc or roller-harrow are made. Fumigant is injected using tractor mounted equipment, followed immediately by several passes with a soil-packing machine. Recently, Telone II™ has been used as the fumigation material, giving excellent control of nematodes. Because of labeling problems, other materials such as methyl bromide and Basamid™ are being used. The field is lightly irrigated after fumigation to seal the soil surface. After 7 to 10 days, the field is disked, fluffed, and allowed to "air-out" before planting. Fields are also limed with 2–4 tons per acre to increase the soil calcium level.

Most of the equipment for planting and digging operations is custom-built by each grower. Complexity and capacity varies by size of operation. All planting and digging operations occur in the period of mid-August to late-October, depending on grower and year.

For planting, rows are formed by tractor, and planting stock is dropped into each row. Individual bulbs are oriented (roots-down) in the row by hand, then covered to 4.5 in. depth for scales and bulblets, and 4.5–5 in. depth for yearlings. Bulbs are then covered and fertilized, usually at the rate of 100–130 lbs. nitrogen per acre.

Lilies naturally flower in mid-July in northern California, and fields of Easter or hybrid lilies are a spectacular sight (Figs. 5 and 6, color plates). Now, however, most flower buds are removed well before flowering. By removing small buds, the plant's energy is diverted into bulb growth, thereby increasing bulb size. Buds can be removed manually or by chemical spray.

Diggers are essentially modified after potato machinery. Bulbs are lifted by an underground blade as the tractor passes along the row. With yearlings and commercials, the green stems usually are removed before digging by a "topper" machine. Bulbs are than carried up onto a conveyor that allows soil to drop to the ground, the bulbs fall into field lugs or bins, and then they are transported to a packing shed for further processing. Figures 7a–f (color plates) show several of these operations in progress.

Indoor Operations

A major indoor operation is the sorting of planting material according to size (circumference) within each bulb age. Many types of equipment are available to mechanize the process, and the efficiency of this process has improved considerably in recent years. Consistent sorting early in the growth cycle is important to speed packing operations in following years. For example, yearling bulbs may be sorted into three to four size sub-classes before replanting. All planting stock (bulblets, scalets, or yearlings) is dipped in a Benlate™/Terraclor™ mixture, then transported back to the field for planting. Every effort must be made to minimize the time out of the ground and to prevent drying of planting stock since bulbs are never truly dormant, and excessive moisture loss reduces quality.

Commercial (saleable) bulbs are brought to sheds, and processed according to size. Bulbs are sorted initially on a weight grader, using the principle that larger bulbs are heavier than smaller ones. This provides some mechanization and efficiency in the initial sort. Eventually, however, each bulb is manually sized and packed into wood or fiber crates with moist peat moss. Crates are stenciled with the cultivar, size (inches circumference), and bulb count. Easter lily bulbs are packed as follows: 6–7 in., 300; 7–8 in., 250; 8–9 in., 200; 9–10 in., 150; 10+ in., 125.

After packing, additional peat moss is added to allow for settling during shipment, and a lid is stapled and strapped to the box. Moisture content of the peat is critical for uniform forcing, and is carefully monitored throughout the shipping period. Packed boxes are held in the shed (common storage) until shipment. Temperatures are not regulated during common storage. Most of the time, however, the prevailing maritime climate in the region favors a relatively constant temperature in packing sheds near 60°–65°F. This temperature allows additional leaf primordia to be initiated in the bulb until vernalization begins. If high temperatures occur at this point, bulbs may be susceptible to sprouting, a problem that is exacerbated with delays in shipping or the start of cold treatment.

Cases are loaded onto trucks and transported to the final greenhouse forcer, or to one of several cold storage (vernalization) facilities in the United States.

Environmental Factors During Shipping

Lily bulbs require oxygen for respiration as does any other living commodity. Systematic studies of bulb respiration have not been carried out, and we do not have clear guidelines concerning required oxygen levels or damaging carbon dioxide levels for lily bulbs. It has been reported that relatively brief periods (14 days) of high CO_2 and low oxygen environments will cause severe bulb damage and ruin the bulb for forcing (Green 1934). More recent information suggests Easter lily bulbs may be tolerant of low oxygen or high CO_2 atmospheres before, during, or after vernalization (Prince and Cunningham 1991). This underlies the importance of moisture content, porosity of the packing medium, and bulb respiration and air exchange in lily packing crates.

Pests of Field Bulb Production

Currently, nematodes and *Botrytis* are the major limitations to field bulb production. Control is mainly through soil fumigation (methyl bromide or Basamid™). *Botrytis* is controlled with sprays of bordeaux, Daconil™, or Kocide™.

The Future

Similar to many aspects of floriculture, the major obstacle facing bulb growers is the tightening of regulations concerning the use of pesticides and other agricultural chemicals. To help with this problem, the Easter Lily Research Foundation, funded by Pacific Northwest growers, is supporting research to help in the registration process for new materials. While this effort is perhaps helpful in the short term, it is inevitable that most current chemicals will eventually be unavailable for field use. Although biological control could be very important in future bulb production schemes, serious biocontrol research has not been conducted.

A breeding program continues at the Foundation Research Facility in Harbor, Oregon. Increased resistance to pests, both during bulb production and during forcing, can be expected in the future. Indeed, genetic resistance to biotic and abiotic stresses may be the ultimate solution to the question of agricultural pesticides in this crop.

Greenhouse Production of Easter Lilies

Cultivars

Presently, 'Nellie White' and 'Ace' are the major cultivars in the United States, comprising about 80–85% and 15–20% of the crop, respectively. The two cultivars are compared in Table 1. New cultivars, bred by a bulb grower-supported program at the research center at Harbor, Oregon, are evaluated yearly at university locations in the United States. Primary breeding objectives have been the development of shorter, earlier-flowering plants with good flower count. Increased flower size is also desirable. Superimposed on a desirable greenhouse plant are the necessary field characteristics: disease and nematode resistance, and, most importantly, ease of propagation and general adaptability to field culture.

Vernalization and Floral Initiation

The Easter lily bulb is never dormant, as in the case of herbaceous perennials or woody plants in the winter. New scales and leaves are formed year-round. When exposed to a favorable environment, a lily bulb will sprout, form leaves, and, at some point, flower.

The primary means of influencing flower forma-

19

tion and timing of flowering is by *vernalization*, or cold-moist treatment prior to greenhouse forcing. Smith (1963) first identified the cold requirement in Easter lily as vernalization. Vernalization predisposes a plant to form flowers and accelerates the flowering process (Table 2). With a normally vernalized Easter lily, flower initiation occurs in mid- to late January when plants are 3–5 in. tall. Vernalization requires cool, moist (but not wet) conditions and an aerobic atmosphere.

What temperatures are "vernalizing" temperatures? The answer to this question came after two decades of active research at Beltsville, Maryland, by the late Dr. Neil Stuart, and by Tom Weiler and Bob Langhans at Cornell University. Through this and other work, we now know that vernalization has two aspects: a qualitative one (does the plant flower or not?) and a quantitative one (how long does it take to flower?). Through their work, it was recognized that temperatures above 70°F (21°C) are non-vernalizing: if the bulb is never exposed to temperatures below 70°F (and the plant is always kept in short days), it will never flower, and will continue to form hundreds of leaves.

Although all temperatures below 70°F are vernalizing, temperatures in the range of 38°–45°F are most effective for vernalization. Recommended vernalization temperatures are as follows: 'Ace', 38°–40°F (3.3°–4.4°C); 'Nellie White', 40°–45°F (4.4°–7.2°C); other cultivars or cultivar mixtures, 40°F. If both cultivars are being grown and only one cooler is available, 40°F is the best compromise temperature. Temperatures below 35°F (1.7°C) severely reduce the rate of vernalization, and bulbs should not be exposed to such low temperatures under normal situations.

The implications of vernalization for the commercial Easter lily grower are shown in Figure 8. Clearly, the number of weeks of vernalization has a significant effect both on the number of flowers and on forcing time. Six

Table 1. Comparison of the major cultivars, 'Nellie White' and 'Ace' (Miller, 1985).

1. Height. 'Nellie White' is shorter than 'Ace'.
2. Bud count. 'Ace' usually has about one more bud than 'Nellie White', within a given bulb size.
3. Forcing time. No consistent differences between these cultivars. 'Nellie White' usually emerges later, but makes up for it after emergence.
4. Leaf number. 'Nellie White' has fewer leaves for bulbs vernalized in the same manner.
5. Flower size. 'Nellie White' has slightly larger flowers, and a larger flower diameter.
6. A-Rest™ tolerance. 'Nellie White' is more susceptible to induced leaf yellowing from growth regulator applications.
7. Vernalization temperature. 'Nellie White' has an optimum of 45°F (7.2°C), while 'Ace' is optimum at 40°F (4.4°C).
8. Leaf scorch from fluorine. Relative to older, obsolete cultivars, both 'Nellie White' and 'Ace' are resistant, and scorch is an uncommon problem in modern production. Even so, 'Ace' is somewhat more susceptible.
9. Fertilizer requirements. Identical for each cultivar.
10. Space requirement. Identical for each cultivar.
11. Timing and development after visible bud. No difference between cultivars. Thus, the same "bud stick" is used.
12. Plant "toughness." 'Ace' is a tougher plant, and is more tolerant of stress, including temperature fluctuations, root rot, and fertilizer problems.
13. Plant picture. 'Nellie White' has distinctly wider and thicker leaves. Well-grown plants of each cultivar, however, have good consumer appeal.

Table 2. Effects of vernalization (cold treatment) on plant characteristics.

1. Reduces the number of flowers and leaves.
2. Reduces the number of days to emergence.
3. Reduces the number of days to anthesis.
4. Reduces the overall height of the plant.
5. Alters plant shape, causing reduced lower leaf length.
6. Improves crop uniformity by reducing variability in emergence and flowering dates.

weeks (1000 hr.) of cooling is recommended for the best compromise in flowering speed, bud count, and final plant quality.

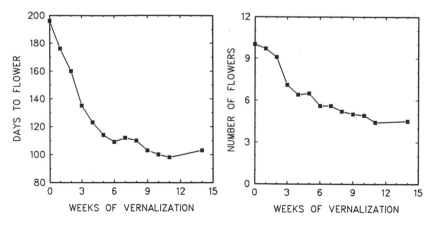

Figure 8. Effect of length of vernalization on days to flower in the greenhouse and number of flowers. In essence, as the cooling period is lengthened, the time to flower is reduced, but at the expense of flower number.

Methods

Four major methods of vernalizing Easter lilies are presently used: 1) "natural cooling," 2) commercial case-cooling, 3) home case-cooling, and 4) "pot-cooling," or controlled-temperature forcing (CTF). Each has advantages and disadvantages, and are outlined below.

NATURAL COOLING
Non-cooled bulbs are potted upon arrival. Potted bulbs should be watered well and never allowed to dry out. Pots are placed in sheds or covered frames, or minimally heated plastic structures, and exposed to the prevailing cool temperatures of October, November, and December. Since accurate temperature control is usually

22

lacking in the cold frame, the specific temperatures given in the previous section cannot be met. It is important, however, that bulb temperatures of 35°–45°F be maintained as best as possible. Records should be kept on minimum and maximum temperatures and duration to provide a guide. Because day temperatures above 70°F are common in central California in late September and early October, split cooling can be useful. After planting, pots are placed in a cooler for the first three weeks, then moved outside for the last three weeks. This is a good compromise if cooler space and time is at a premium. Assuming enough cooling has occurred (1000 hr. near 40°F), pots are moved into the greenhouse about 120 days before the scheduled bloom date.

Greenhouse temperatures should be maintained at 60°–65°F (15.5°–18°C) until emergence and flower initiation. Lower temperatures cause slow initial growth, and also continue to vernalize the bulbs, resulting in reduced flower number. One of the advantages of natural cooling is that the outdoor period allows some roots to form prior to greenhouse forcing. This is advantageous during subsequent forcing because the bulb does not have to produce a root and shoot system simultaneously. With this method, the length of lower foliage is increased, and rapid initial shoot elongation is reduced. Both of these factors improve final plant shape. The basic problem with natural cooling, however, is the lack of adequate temperature control during the cooling phase. Without sufficient cooling, plants take too long to force and are taller. Also, this method is only possible where the grower is certain the bulbs will not be allowed to freeze.

COMMERCIAL CASE-COOLING

In this situation, the grower receives bulbs that have been vernalized in the case at a commercial cold storage facility. The vernalized bulbs should be potted immediately upon arrival from the supplier, about 110–

120 days before Easter. After potting, they should be watered well and placed in the greenhouse. Warm soil temperature [63°–65°F (17°–18.5°C)] should be maintained if forcing time is limited. After about three weeks, roots should be visible to the edge of the root ball, and the shoot should be emerging. Nighttime greenhouse temperature should be lowered to 60°F (15.5°C) at this point. If enough forcing time is available, plants can be started cooler [55°–58°F (12.8°–14.4°C)] to improve rooting before shoot growth occurs. "Insurance lighting" ("mum lighting" to provide interrupted nights) may be used if insufficient cooling is suspected (see below). If cooled properly, plants should flower in 120 days at 60°F night temperatures.

The primary advantage of commercial case-cooling is its simplicity. Bulbs have theoretically been fully treated, and the grower has only to pot the bulbs and move them into the greenhouse. On the other hand, there is still an inherent lack of control in this method. The grower truly has no assurances of the actual temperature or duration of the cold treatment, or that unusual temperature fluctuations did not occur in the storage environment. Many shippers are now using sealed temperature recorders to document temperatures bulbs were exposed to during shipping and storage. While this is good evidence if problems occur in storage, by the time bulbs arrive it is usually too late to correct these major problems.

HOME CASE-COOLING

This method allows the grower complete control over the storage and vernalization temperature of the bulbs and eliminates the problems noted above. The procedure is possible only if the grower has a well-maintained, accurately controlled cooler of sufficient size to handle the quantity of bulbs to be forced. Cases of non-cooled bulbs are placed in the cooler upon receipt, at these temperatures: 'Ace', 38°–40°F (3.3°–4.4°C); 'Nellie White',

40°–45°F (4.4°–7.2°C); other cultivars or cultivar mixtures, 40°F (4.4°C). Growers must monitor bulb temperature by using thermometers inserted into the center of several cases, and adjust the cooler thermostat to maintain the recommended bulb temperatures. Seven to 10 days may be necessary for bulbs in the center of the packing cases to reach 40°F after placement of cases in cold storage (Langhans and Weiler 1967). In the vast majority of the Easter lilies forced in the United States, this time lag is not accounted for in cooling schedules. This oversight could be a major source of the variability seen in lily crops, although no direct published information exists to support or refute this claim.

Additionally, home case-cooling gives the grower the opportunity to better control the moisture content of the packing case. Due to bulb respiration requirements, cases are well ventilated, and often peat in the outer part of the case will dry out. Since vernalization is a process requiring moisture, bulbs in case periphery may receive less vernalization than required. To overcome this situation, 1–2 quarts of water can be added to the top of each case, usually after 2–3 weeks of storage. Also, the outsides of cases may be sprayed with water and loosely covered with polyethylene to maintain moisture in the cases.

The use of internal polyethylene case liners was advocated long ago by Stuart (1954) and more recently by Prince and Cunningham (1990). Polyethylene is permeable to oxygen, nitrogen, and carbon dioxide, but allows little water vapor to pass. Bulbs from cases with poly liners emerged more uniformly than bulbs from non-lined cases, but only at the lowest peat moisture content tested. In other words, poly liners are good if the peat dries out, but are not necessary if the peat is kept moist. Also, research demonstrated that flowering was accelerated in lined cases, suggesting more efficient cold perception due to moister conditions. Even with these benefits, the use of poly lined cases has not been widely adopted for Easter lily packing primarily because of poor results obtained with commercial poly liner trials in the mid-1960s. In these trials, the peat was too moist and many bulbs rotted.

After cooling is complete, bulbs are potted as described above for commercially case-cooled bulbs. Daily temperature records during storage should be kept and maintained.

"POT-COOLING," OR CONTROLLED TEMPERATURE FORCING (CTF)

This method is based on research conducted by Stuart (1967), Merritt (1963), and De Hertogh et al. (1969). Typical responses to CTF are greater flower bud numbers and increased length of lower foliage. Also, greenhouse forcing time (after cooling) is reduced by about 7 to 10 days, as compared to other methods given the same amount of cooling. These responses are undoubtedly due to the increased root mass available to support early shoot and leaf growth after the cooling period. This method has the greatest potential to produce the highest quality plants. On the other hand, pot-cooling is the most labor and physical-plant intensive, and requires a greater attention to detail than the other three methods.

Basically, non-cooled bulbs are potted, irrigated, and given three weeks of warm [63°F (17°C)] temperatures to promote root growth prior to the cooling period. The soil must be kept moist, but not wet, at all times. After three weeks, pots are moved to a cooler and held for six weeks at these temperatures: 'Ace', 38°–40°F (3.3°–4.4°C); 'Nellie White', 40°–45°F (4.4°–7.2°C); other cultivars or cultivar mixtures, 40°F. Soil temperature should be monitored, and accurate records kept for future use. About 110 days prior to desired flowering, pots are brought into the greenhouse. For the first four to six weeks, soil temperatures should be maintained at about 60°–65°F (15.5°–18°C). Thereafter, 60°F (15.5°C) night temperatures are used until leaf counting begins.

It is important to consider the length of the 63°F rooting period in early-Easter years. If forcing schedules are tight, it is necessary to sacrifice the rooting period, but *not* the length of vernalization. The critical time span is the six weeks of vernalization. If full vernalization is not achieved, the plants will flower later, and it will be extremely difficult to flower the crop on time.

Insurance Lighting

If bulbs are suspected of having less than six weeks of vernalization, "insurance policy" lighting is recommended, especially in early-Easter years (Table 3). After emergence, long photoperiods substitute for vernalization, with exactly the same effects, i.e., reduction in leaf and flower number, and reductions in days to flower. Lighting is most effective within the two-week period at and just after emergence. Best results are obtained through the use

Table 3. Easter dates until the year 2013 (*Catholic Almanac* 1989).

1990	April 15	2002	March 31
1991	March 31	2003	April 20
1992	April 19	2004	April 11
1993	April 11	2005	March 27
1994	April 3	2006	April 16
1995	April 16	2007	April 8
1996	April 7	2008	March 23
1997	March 30	2009	April 12
1998	April 12	2010	April 4
1999	April 4	2011	April 24
2000	April 23	2012	April 8
2001	April 15	2013	March 31

Easter date classification
Early: March 22 to April 2
Medium: April 3 to April 15
Late: April 15 to April 25

of night break lighting from 10 PM to 2 AM. Lights should remain on for only the amount of time to make up for lost cold treatment, up to two weeks. This will provide the equivalent of up to two weeks of vernalization to the crop. Since there will be variation in actual dates of emergence, some sorting of pots can be done to provide a relatively uniform lighting period to the whole crop. Some growers believe that later emerging plants have fewer leaves, require fewer days to force, and therefore need fewer days of insurance lighting than earlier emerging plants. This has not been confirmed experimentally.

Insurance policy lighting should not be done in late-Easter years, unless a major disruption occurred in bulb cold storage. With proper (six weeks) cold storage *and* two weeks of insurance lighting, plants flower too early, leading to major problems in trying to hold plants in coolers prior to sale.

Bulb Size

Bulbs are available in a range of sizes (circumferences). Generally, the larger the bulb, the more leaves and flowers will be formed on the plant, and the taller it will be (Table 4) (Blaney et al. 1965; Langhans and Smith

Table 4. Effects of bulb size on forcing time, number of flowers, and height in Easter lily (Langhans and Smith 1966).

Bulb circumference (in.)	Days to flower	Number of flowers	Height (in.)
6–7	102	2.7	12.4
7–8	102	3.2	14.0
8–9	102	5.0	18.0
9–10	96	6.0	18.0
10–up	97	5.1	18.4

1966). Larger bulbs tend to force a bit faster than smaller ones. Generally, growers use large bulbs (8 in. or larger) to produce the highest quality crops. Since larger bulbs produce taller plants with more leaves, they should be given slightly more space (an additional 10–12%) than smaller bulbs for maximum quality.

MERISTEM DIAMETER

Larger bulbs have larger apical meristems, and this is probably the main reason for increased flower numbers. Pot cooling (controlled temperature forcing), which increases flower number, also tends to increase meristem diameter (De Hertogh et al. 1976). Also, it has long been known that the rate of leaf initiation and unfolding is positively correlated to apex diameter (Kohl 1967; Lange and Heins 1990). Using an 8–9 in. bulb as a standard, 6–7 in., and 10+ in. bulbs will have about a 15% decrease or increase (respectively) in leaf unfolding rate.

Storage for Late Easters

Work in the 1940s and 1950s (Stuart 1952) first demonstrated that bulb freezing [31°–28°F (−0.5° to −2°C)] was useful for long-term holding of bulbs prior to planting. Since freezing reduces the rate of vernalization, the deleterious effects of over-vernalization (for example, reduction in bud count) are also reduced. This is the basis of bulb storage for year-round forcing of Oriental and Asiatic hybrids, as discussed later. Bulb freezing, however, has not been used for potted Easter lilies because Easter lilies are much less tolerant of freezing than Oriental and Asiatic hybrids.

In late-Easter years and in warm growing areas, such as Arizona, where lily forcing time is greatly accelerated, it may be that bulb freezing could be used to delay planting for one to two weeks. A better method to delay planting, however, is to simply reduce cooler temperatures to just above freezing [32°–34°F (0°–1.1°C)] after about four to five weeks of normal vernalization temperatures.

Scheduling

OVERVIEW
Greenhouse forcing is usually divided into three phases:

    I. Planting to flower bud initiation
      a. Planting to emergence
      b. Emergence to flower bud initiation
    II. Flower bud initiation to visible bud
    III. Visible bud to flowering.

In all cases, temperature is the overriding control over the rate of plant growth and development, and of final plant quality. Photoperiod (insurance lighting) can play a substantial role in the first phase, before flower initiation.

EASTER DATES
Easter falls on the first Sunday following the full moon that occurs on or after the vernal (spring) equinox. Since the vernal equinox occurs on March 21, Easter can occur from March 22 to April 25 (*Webster's Third* 1981). Easter dates until 2013 are given in Table 3 (*Catholic Almanac* 1989).

One of the major scheduling considerations is the desired visible bud date. The visible bud stage is defined as the time when buds are visible at the shoot apex without having to move the last few young leaves away from the buds. At visible bud, the young buds are about 0.5–1 in. long. Generally, plan on 35–42 days (5–6 weeks) to bring plants into flower, depending on forcing temperature.

PHASE I. PLANTING TO FLOWER BUD INITIATION
In this phase, the bulb is producing roots and becoming established in the pot. Early shoot growth is occurring, followed by shoot emergence. Since the bulb and non-emerged shoot are surrounded by the potting mix, soil temperature is the key environmental factor. After shoot emergence, the plant becomes responsive to air temperatures, and DIF management can be started. Flowers form (initiate) when the shoot is about 3–5 in. tall (mid- to late January, depending on the year). Stem roots are visible starting with FBI and are a non-destructive indicator of flower initiation.

After potting, use 60°–62°F soil temperatures until emergence. For slow emerging crops, first try 2°–3°F higher. Even soil temperatures as high as 70°F should be okay as long as bulbs have been fully vernalized. There is always the question of "de-vernalization," or erasure of vernalization accumulation by high temperatures before and during the time of crop emergence. In the de-vernalization research of the 1960s (Miller and Kiplinger 1966a, 1966b; Weiler and Langhans 1972), researchers found that 70°F or above can, in some cases, erase the effects of previous cold storage. They found that warm temperature interruption in the first two weeks of the six-week cold period is more effective in erasing vernalization than is a warm period in the last two weeks of the cold period. That is, de-vernalization due to 70°F soil temperatures up to and during emergence should not occur with fully vernalized bulbs. Even so, the danger of de-vernalization does become greater with higher temperatures. As an extreme example, using 85° or 90°F soil temperatures to force shoot emergence will certainly lead to de-vernalization, as well as other physiological problems. These problems point to the advantages of home case-cooling or pot-cooling where better control and assurance of storage temperature is possible.

After emergence, use 60°–62°F until flower initia-

31

tion. High temperatures after emergence and during flower initiation will reduce bud count.

Greenhouse temperature "dip". It has been reported that lowering greenhouse temperatures during the flower bud initiation phase (late January to early February) can result in an increase in bud count (Wilkins and Roh 1977; R. O. Miller, personal communication). Night temperatures of 45°–50°F (60°F days) for 7–14 days during flower initiation are effective for both 'Ace' and 'Nellie White'. Presumably, lower temperatures allow formation of additional flower buds because of the increased meristematic dome area that is caused by the reduced developmental rate.

The major problem with temperature dipping is the necessity to accurately time the low temperature treatment to occur during flower initiation. This requires dissection of some plants. Temperature dipping *after* flower bud initiation has no beneficial effect on bud count. Temperature dipping is best used for late Easters, and for growers who are leaf counting (see below) so that sufficient time remains for crop forcing after the dip. Growers who have no experience with this technique should first experiment on a small scale to obtain experience with scheduling and plant response. In no case should plants experience high temperatures (65°F or above) during flower initiation. Reduced bud count will result.

PHASE II. FBI TO VISIBLE BUD (VB)

In this phase, flowers continue to grow and develop from microscopic primordia into visible buds about 0.5–1 in. long. Buds "become visible" because the leaves surrounding them grow, and the leaf tips unfold away from the stem apex (meristem) where the buds have initiated. In addition to leaf unfolding, about half of the plant height is developed during this time. All crops should be timed after flower bud initiation by the leaf counting technique detailed below.

Leaf counting. The Easter lily is a determinate plant; that is, when the terminal apex becomes reproductive, no more leaves are formed. This determinate characteristic allows growers to begin accurate crop timing quite early in the crop. The procedure requires that several plants be sacrificed in late January, after microscopic flowers form in the apex. Interestingly, the Easter lily begins to form stem roots at about the same time as it is forming flowers. By scraping a little soil away from the stem the presence of stem roots can be noted. This is a good nondestructive way to see monitor flower initiation. After flower initiation starts, the number of leaves is fixed, and may be determined by dissection and counting leaves. Based on this result, greenhouse temperatures are manipulated to control the rate of additional leaf unfolding until visible bud. Details of leaf counting are given below:

1. Around January 15 to 20, randomly select 5–10 plants of each major lot of bulbs. "Lots" are different cultivars, bulb sizes, bulb sources, or growing areas. Do not count earlier than mid-January because plants will still be vegetative, and flower buds will not be present.
2. Mark with a pen or hole punch the youngest "unfolded" leaf. An unfolded leaf is one that has bent away from the "spindle" of younger, vertical leaves. Usually, the leaf tip must unfold 45 degrees to be counted (Fig. 9).
3. Starting with the bottom leaves, count all unfolded leaves, up to and including the leaf marked in step 2. Record this number in a column labeled "unfolded leaves."
4. Now, count the remaining small leaves ("leaves to unfold"). After a point, it will be necessary to use a needle and dissecting microscope or good hand lens. Continue counting all leaves until the growing point is reached. Tiny buds should be visible (Fig. 10). If so, then the plant is reproductive, and the number of leaves to unfold can be recorded. At this time, you can also get an early idea of bud count. If buds are not present, the plant was still vegetative and the leaf count should be disregarded. If other plants are also vegetative, wait a few days, and repeat the procedure.

5. Add the number of "unfolded" leaves and "leaves to unfold" to determine the total number of leaves. An example may be as follows:

Leaves unfolded:	34
Leaves to unfold:	58
Total leaves:	92

6. Repeat this for several other plants in the lot, and average the numbers together. These numbers (especially the number of young, folded leaves) are the basis of the leaf counting procedure.

A

B
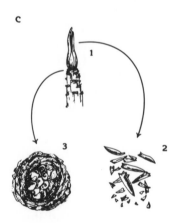

C
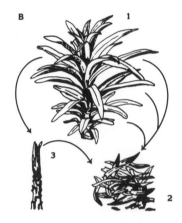

A. Example of stage of growth on Easter lily in late January.

B. 1. Excised shoot in late January.

   2. Unfolded leaves removed.

   3. Lost leaf unfolded off spindle.

C. 1. A shoot in late January with leaves that have to be unfolded off meristem until buds visible date.

   2. Leaves to be unfolded.

   3. Topographical view of shoot meristem with initiated flowers in the center and leaf base on the periphery.

Figure 9. Leaf counting of Easter lilies. (Kindly provided by G. De Hertogh and J. Love, North Carolina State University, Raleigh, N.C.).

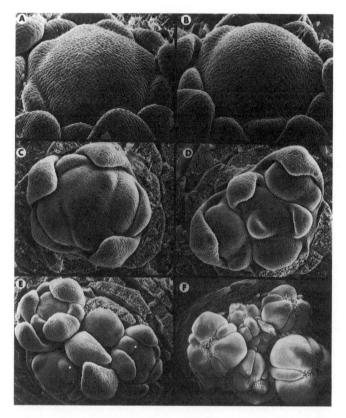

Figure 10. Phases in flower bud initiation in Easter lily. (Reprinted from *J. Amer. Soc. Hort. Sci.* 101:463–471, 1976, A. A. De Hertogh, H. P., Rasmussen, and N. Blakely.)

Timing with leaf counting. Once the number of leaves to be unfolded is determined, the degree of forcing difficulty is established. The immature leaves must be unfolded in the time between the leaf counting date and the desired visible bud date. With many leaves to be unfolded, average forcing temperatures must be higher than if fewer leaves remain to be unfolded. To determine correct forcing temperatures, count back the number of days from Easter that buds should be visible. This is usually five to six weeks before marketing since it takes six weeks to bring a plant into flower from the visible bud stage at 60°F night temperature. Once the VB date is established, determine the number of days between the VB date and the date of leaf counting. This is the number of days available to unfold the remaining leaves (as determined in

35

step 4, above). Suppose that leaf counts were made on January 20, and the desired date of VB is March 1, allowing 40 days to unfold the remaining leaves. From the example above, there are 58 leaves to unfold. Therefore, to have visible bud (i.e., all leaves unfolded) by March 1: 58 leaves/40 days = 1.45 leaves per day (on average) that must be unfolded between January 20 and March 1.

To monitor this rate of leaf unfolding, mark 5–10 average plants from each bulb lot of interest. With a pen or a hole punch, mark the last unfolded leaf, then count the number of leaves unfolded on the same plant. Record this number on a label in the pot. At regular intervals (perhaps every four to six days) count the number of leaves that have unfolded since the last count. Marking the last unfolded leaf each time makes counting easier. Try not to disturb the plants any more than necessary. Dividing this number by the number of days gives the daily rate of leaf unfolding since the last count. If your unfolding rate is greater than the calculated required rate, then greenhouse temperatures may be lowered slightly, and vice-versa.

It is possible to graphically track lily leaf unfolding in the same manner as with height tracking. Mr. Jim Graves of Cottage Gardens Nursery (St. Helena, Calif.) has used this system with great success. The assumption is that leaf unfolding is constant from flower bud initiation to visible bud. On a graph with time along the bottom, plot the number of unfolded leaves at flower initiation and the total number of leaves at visible bud. By connecting these two points, a line is created that gives the number of leaves that should be unfolded at any given time before visible bud. This is essentially a graph of plant development rate and is very useful in temperature management. The next step is to plot height on the bottom axis and number of unfolded leaves along the y axis. This key graph relates plant development (unfolded leaves) to plant height and helps the grower decide whether plants are too tall for their developmental stage and vice-versa.

Table 5 gives estimated rates of leaf unfolding for a range of daily average temperatures. To calculate the average daily temperature in the greenhouse, multiply the day temperature by the number of hours that temperature is maintained. Do the same for night temperature. Add these two totals together, and divide by 24 (hours/day). This gives

Table 5. Leaf unfolding rates as affected by average daily (24-hr.) temperature for 8/9-in. bulbs (Karlsson et al. 1988).

Leaves unfolded per day	Average daily temperature (F°)[1]
1.0	53
1.1	55
1.2	57
1.3	59
1.4	61
1.5	63
1.6	65
1.7	67
1.8	69
1.9	70
2.0	72
2.1	74
2.2	76
2.3	78
2.4	80
2.5	82

[1]Average daily temperature = (day temp. × hours day temp. maintained) + (night temp. × hours night temp. maintained) / 24

the average temperature the plants are exposed to during the 24-hr. period.

From Table 5, it can be seen that an 11-degree temperature increase from 61° to 72°F increases the rate of leaf unfolding by 0.6 leaves per day. Over a five-week period, this is an increase of 21 extra leaves that can be unfolded. Over a one-week period, however, only about four additional leaves can be unfolded. The take-home message is that leaf counting and temperature manipulation must begin immediately after flower initiation is complete. Temperature increases over a long time period are very effective in increasing the rate of lily development, but in the short term are nearly useless.

PHASE III. VISIBLE BUD TO FLOWERING

Figure 11 shows a version of the lily "bud stick," the earliest tool for lily timing. Leaf counting is a relatively new procedure (last 15 years or so), and before leaf counting the bud stick was the only timing device available. The bud stick is used by placing the pointed end at the base of the bud, where it attaches to the plant. At the tip of the bud, the grower reads the number of days for the bud to flower at each of several temperatures. Depending on the developmental stage of the buds, greenhouse temperatures are raised or lowered to increase or reduce flower bud growth.

Temperature manipulation after visible bud must be done with care, however. The greatest "bang for the buck" in terms of forcing speed and temperature comes between 55° and 70°F (12.8° and 21.1°C) (Table 6). While average temperatures above 70°F do cause slightly faster bud development (Roh and Wilkins 1973), it is far better to maintain temperatures a degree or two warmer throughout leaf counting and early development after visible bud than it is to force at 75°F (23.9°C) for a few weeks at the end. For the most part, forcing lilies at temperatures above 70°F wastes fuel and reduces plant quality. It is much more important to keep the crop on track early with leaf counting. Also, height increases significantly in the last six weeks of the forcing period, as discussed in detail later. High temperature forcing, especially with day temperatures greater than nights, results in tall plants. The solution is to avoid high temperature forcing late in the crop.

Table 6. Effect of average temperature on days from visible bud to opening of the first flower (Erwin et al. 1987).

Temperature (°F)	Days VB to flowering	Decrease in days from VB-F due to a 5°F increase
55	42	—
60	38	4
65	34	4
70	31	3
75	27	4
80	25	2
85	24	1

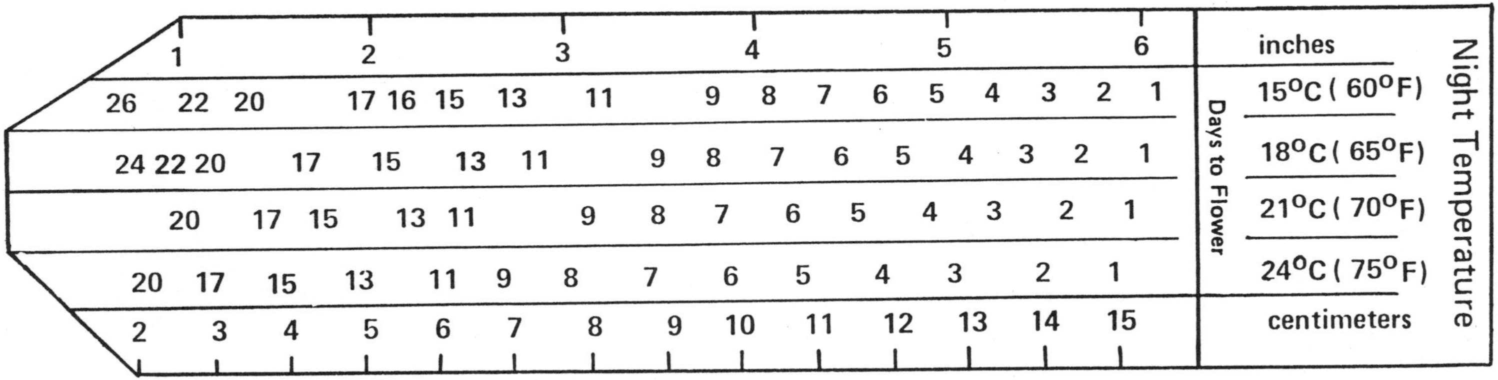

Night Temperature

inches	15°C (60°F)	18°C (65°F)	21°C (70°F)	24°C (75°F)	centimeters
	Days to Flower				
1	26				2
	22 20	24 22 20			3
2	17 16 15	17	20	20	4
	13	15	17 15	17	5
3	11	13 11	13 11	15	6
	9	9	9	11	7
	8	8	8	9	8
4	9 8	7	7	7	9
	7	6	6	6	10
	6	5	5	5	11
5	5	5	4	4	12
	4	4	4	3	13
	3	3	3	2	14
6	2	2	2	1	15
	1	1	1		

Figure 11. The "bud stick," a device used to determine the time required to open flower buds at a given temperature. The stick is used by placing the end against the base of the bud, at the bud base-pedicel junction. At the bud tip, the number of days until flower opening is read for the different temperatures. Note: This bud stick is not printed to scale.

39

Growing Medium

PHYSICAL CHARACTERISTICS

As with nearly all pot plants, three important characteristics are necessary for a lily potting medium: 1) excellent drainage, 2) excellent water-holding capacity, and 3) excellent fertilizer-holding capacity (cation exchange capacity). A growing medium with these characteristics helps to eliminate problems such as root rot, elevated soluble salts, and nutrient deficiencies.

Many growers prefer to incorporate mineral soil into their potting mix. Loamy field soil has excellent nutrient-holding capacity, and adds weight to the pot, a useful characteristic when taller lilies are grown. The drawback to field soil is the potential for disease, weeds, and herbicide injury. If the grower has complete control over the soil source, then the latter considerations can be eliminated. Many growers have been successful using 20–35% (by volume) field soil in their mixes. Some successful mixtures are given in Table 7.

Lilies of excellent quality can also be grown in soilless mixes (Table 7). It is important to remember, however, that peat moss and other organic materials such as bark have very little nutrient-holding capacity (cation exchange capacity) on a volume basis. Also, peat-lite mixes have a low bulk density (weight per pot), and with tall lilies plant stability can be a problem. When media components with a high carbon to nitrogen ratio (e.g., bark or other partially decomposed materials) are used, incorporation of slow release nitrogen (0.5 lb. urea formaldehyde per cubic yd.) is recommended to maintain available nitrogen during bark decomposition (Miller 1985).

CHEMICAL CHARACTERISTICS

It is important to begin the crop with a growing medium containing the proper nutritional properties. Lilies are heavy feeders, and pre-plant fertilizer incorpora-

Table 7. Potting mixes for lilies.

Soil-based mixes

    1:1:1 (by volume) loamy soil, coarse perlite or coarse vermiculite, and coarse peat moss.

    Pre-plant amendments[1]:

Calcium limestone	6 lb./yd.$^{-3}$
Dolomitic limestone	6 lb./yd.$^{-3}$
12-12-12 (or other complete fertilizer)	1 lb./yd.$^{-3}$

Soil-less (peat-lite) mixes

    2:1:1 (by volume) peat moss, coarse vermiculite, and coarse perlite.

    Pre-plant amendments:

Calcium limestone		6 lb./yd.$^{-3}$
Dolomitic limestone		6 lb./yd.$^{-3}$
Gypsum (calcium sulfate)		2 lb./yd.$^{-3}$
Calcium *or* potassium nitrate		1 lb./yd.$^{-3}$
12-12-12 (or other complete fertilizer)		1 lb./yd.$^{-3}$
Trace elements:	Perk™	4 lb./yd.$^{-3}$
or	Esmigran™	4 lb./yd.$^{-3}$
or	or Micro-max™	1.5 lb./yd.$^{-3}$
Superphosphate/treble superphosphate		none

[1]Exact amounts should be based on previous soil test results.

tion, as given in Table 8, is suggested as a starting point. Low nutrition early in the crop will reduce final plant quality. Calcium is especially important for healthy root growth and to prevent leaf scorch. Ideally, growing medium should be tested prior to planting, and amended accordingly. A pH of 6.5 to 7.0 is recommended for soil based mixtures, with soil-less (peat-lite) mixes about 0.3 to 0.6 pH unit lower.

It is difficult to recommend specific ranges of nutrients that should be maintained in the growing medium. Many soil testing facilities use different methods for analysis, and numbers are not usually transferrable between labs. The best policy is to regularly test soils, keep track of the results, and gain confidence and experience with one or two laboratories.

Table 8. Fertilization programs for Easter lilies to supply 200, 300, or 400 ppm nitrogen (Langhans et al. 1990).

ppm nitrogen	Fertilizer source	Proportional ratio used		
		1:200	1:100	1:15
		oz./gal. fertilizer stock solution		
200	Potassium nitrate	14.0	7.0	1.0
	and			
	Calcium nitrate	24.0	12.0	1.8
	OR			
	15-0-15	36.0	18.0	2.7
	OR			
	20-0-20 or 20-10-20	26.7	13.4	2.0
300	Potassium nitrate	21.0	10.5	1.6
	and			
	Calcium nitrate	36.0	18.0	2.7
	OR			
	15-0-15	54.0	27.0	4.1
	OR			
	20-0-20 or 20-10-20	40.1	20.0	3.0
400	Potassium nitrate	28.0	14.0	2.0
	and			
	Calcium nitrate	48.0	24.0	3.6
	OR			
	15-0-15	72.0	36.0	5.4
	OR			
	20-0-20 or 20-10-20	53.4	26.8	4.0
	After flower buds are 0.5 in. long			
200	Calcium nitrate	36.0	18.0	2.7
300	Calcium nitrate	54.0	27.0	4.1
400	Calcium nitrate	72.0	36.0	5.4

There is one major soil characteristic that is easy to measure, and has a profound effect on plant growth, and that is soluble salts or electrical conductivity (EC). Lilies are easily damaged by high levels of soluble salts in the growing medium. Soluble salts come from the growing medium and incorporated fertilizer, from liquid fertilization, and from the irrigation water itself. As the soil mix dries out, the remaining salts become extremely concentrated. Maintain salts less than 3.5 mmho/cm in a saturated paste extract, or 2.0 mmho/cm in a 1:2 (medium:water) extract. If salts rise above these levels, a thorough leaching with clear water will dissolve and wash salts away.

GROWTH MEDIUM AND LEAF SCORCH

Soil chemical characteristics play a major role in *leaf scorch*, a physiological disorder that is generally attributed to fluoride. The cultivar 'Nellie White' is more resistant to leaf scorch than is 'Ace', while 'Croft', an old cultivar, was devastated by leaf scorch. In fact, the old advice for avoiding leaf scorch on 'Croft' was to grow 'Ace' instead! More information on leaf scorch is given in the "Physiological Disorders" section.

Several fluoride sources occur in the greenhouse. Fluoride-containing acids are used during the manufacture of superphosphate, and this fertilizer should be used with caution for lily forcing. Perlite and fluoridated municipal water also have appreciable levels of fluoride.

Since phosphorus is an essential nutrient, however, some phosphorus must be available during growth. Research at Cornell University has demonstrated that 0.5 lb. superphosphate per cubic yd. is safe if the pH is maintained at 6.8 to 7.2. Monocalcium phosphate does not contain fluoride and can be added at 0.67 lb. per cubic yd. It is useful if water pH is acidic, as growth medium pH will tend to decrease over time. Soluble phosphorus fertilizers (e.g., 20-10-20) do not contain damaging levels of fluoride and are convenient to use. Food grade phosphoric acid (75%) is used by many growers to acidify irrigation water and is an excellent fluoride-free phosphorus source. Ammonium fertilizers can cause reductions in soil pH, and thus increase incidence of scorch (Marousky and Woltz 1977).

Fortunately, leaf scorch is an easily controlled problem. The cultivar 'Nellie White' is highly resistant to scorch. With higher soil pHs, fluoride is less available and causes less damage (Marousky and Woltz 1977). A soil-based media pH of 6.8 to 7.2 (slightly less for soil-less mixes) essentially eliminates leaf scorch as a production problem. Thus, adequate lime should be incorporated into the mix before potting. The exact amount needed should be determined by a soil test. With proper pH control, perlite (at least up to one-third of the volume) causes no leaf scorch problem.

Planting

Bulbs should be planted at the appropriate time, as described in the vernalization section. Planting of case-cooled bulbs must not be delayed, as the bulbs will sprout in the case. This leads to direct injury to the emerging shoots, as well as the likelihood of lower stems being devoid of foliage.

Full-depth ("standard") pots are strongly recommended (not "azalea" or "¾" pots). Deeper pots allow better drainage, and therefore reduce incidence of root rot. Bulbs should be planted so that the top of the bulb is about 2 in. below the soil line, with about 1 in. of soil below the bulb. This ensures the bulb is above the water saturation zone of the pot and also allows adequate soil above the bulb for stem roots to develop. Firm, but do not pack, medium around and over the bulb. The top of the soil should be about 0.5 in. below the pot rim to allow application of enough water to completely wet the growing medium during irrigation.

Before good height control measures were available, growers used to place gravel in the bottom of the pot to provide weight and stability. This should *not* be done. This practice reduces the height of the soil column, reducing drainage from the pot. Increased root rot could result.

Bulbs that are sprouted should be planted on their side, and the sprout carefully bent to emerge near the center of the pot. With sprouted bulbs, cover the etiolated (white) part of the stem with soil, and be sure the shoot is not damaged. The use of shorter, "azalea" pots lead to especially poor performance with sprouted bulbs because of lack of drainage and soil volume for stem rooting. After planting, pots should be watered two to three times in succession to ensure complete wetting of the planting mixture. Use of spray stakes or otherwise gentle sprinkler irrigation is preferred over heavy drenching to avoid soil compaction.

Fungicide Drenches

Plants should be given a preventative fungicide treatment within one to three days after planting for control of the root rot complex. Primary organisms involved in this very serious disease are: *Rhizoctonia*, *Pythium*, *Phytopthora*, and *Cylindrocarpon*. Fungicides must be rotated for effective control, and to avoid plant injury. Details of chemical control are found in the "Insect Pests and Diseases" section.

Irradiance

Lilies are a high light crop and require the maximum amount of light possible for Easter forcing. The grower should be aware of overhead structures such as yellowed greenhouse coverings, piping, shade cloth bundles, and equipment. All reduce light and are detrimental to crop quality. It must be emphasized that low light intensity is one of the major factors affecting height in lilies, and all efforts to increase greenhouse light will keep plants shorter and improve quality (see also the "Height Control" section).

Irrigation

Thorough irrigation immediately after potting is crucial for uniform emergence and crop establishment. Later, during growth, an evenly moist growth medium encourages rooting and development of lush, high-quality foliage.

Pots should be irrigated so that about 10–15% of the applied water leaches out of the pot. This reduces salt accumulation within the growing medium. However, with the likelihood of increased governmental regulation of runoff from commercial greenhouses, the present methods of watering and fertilizing must be re-examined and changed. Research into the use of flood benches, recirculating water, or other environmentally sound techniques is necessary.

It is worth experimenting with ebb and flow benches for Easter lilies, and the results may be pleasing. In 1985, we grew 'Nellie White' lilies in a recirculating hydroponic system at Cornell University. About 300 plants were grown using several troughs and a common 30-gallon nutrient solution reservoir. For root rot control, a Lesan™ drench was applied, and allowed to run out of the system. No root pathogen problems were seen, and the tops and roots were of excellent quality (Fig. 12, color plates).

The amount of water a plant requires depends on: 1) the size of the plant, 2) the air and soil temperature, 3) the light level in the greenhouse, 4) the amount of air movement in the greenhouse, 5) the relative humidity, and 6) other factors. It is easy to envision the dark, cold days of early February, when houses are tightly closed with little air movement. Under these conditions, plant transpiration rate is low, and less frequent watering is needed. If liquid feed is used, nitrogen deficiency is often apparent at this time because of lack of irrigation, and supplemental N application is useful (see the "Nutrition and Fertilization" section).

Over-watering results in direct root injury and the likelihood of increased root rot problems. In fact, severe over-watering, in which the soil never dries, results in 100% flower bud blast and severely stunted growth (Tincker 1950; Miller and Langhans 1986).

The method of irrigation is extremely important. Automatic "spaghetti" and capillary mat systems result in taller lilies than does hand watering. Several explanations can be made for this. First, overhead watering will lead to cooler leaves as the water evaporates. Second, the mechanical stress of water droplets hitting the leaves probably causes a slight increase in ethylene formation, with a result of slightly reduced growth. That mechanical stress leads to shorter lilies has been known in the scientific literature for a long time (Hiraki and Ota 1975). Mechanical stress certainly has not been adopted as a component in lily height management but deserves more study. Water temperature can also play a role in height control, with lilies finishing progressively shorter as irrigation water temperature falls from 65° to 35°F (Peterson and Kramer 1990).

While many smaller growers are able to hand irrigate their crops, many larger growers rely on a "spray-stake" type of system. These systems are also useful for moistening foliage on hot spring days, late in the crop cycle. Such syringing helps reduce leaf temperature and "holds the plants back." With water high in dissolved solids, spray stakes will leave deposits on the leaves, reducing final plant quality.

A full discussion of water quality is beyond the scope of this book. Much information on water quality and alkalinity has been disseminated through the Ohio State University Water Survey conducted in the early to mid-1980s (Peterson and Kramer 1990), and from commercial analytical laboratories (Anon. 1988). The concept of water alkalinity and long-term growing medium pH change is an important one in greenhouse crop production. Water should be analyzed, and provisions made for water acidification, if necessary.

Nutrition and Fertilization

Lilies are heavy feeders, and best growth comes with a program of both soil-incorporated and regular liquid fertilization. A "starting point" fertilization program is given in Table 8. In greenhouses with soft water or low soil pH, use of calcium nitrate is preferable after buds are 0.5 in. long. The extra calcium is important to healthy roots, to bud growth, and for reducing fluoride-induced leaf scorch.

Because of high rates of fertilization, growers should check for salt accumulation, and leach the soil if necessary. If 10–15% of the volume of applied fertilizer water leaches through the soil and drains from the pot, usually no salt problem will occur. Electrical conductivity (EC) readings above 3.5 mmho/cm (saturated paste) or 2.0 mmho/cm for a 1:2 (medium:water) extract indicate that leaching is necessary. An electrical conductivity meter is a relatively inexpensive piece of equipment that every greenhouse operation should have. High salts lead to root injury, stunted plants, and eventually to yellowed lower leaves which do not recover. Test soil salts once each week, and record results. A chart can be prepared with time on the lower axis and salts reading on the upper axis. By plotting EC and events such as irrigation, fertilization, and leaching, a better understanding of soil salt accumulation will be gained. Chronically low readings could mean more frequent fertilization is needed, that the injector is not working properly, or that stock solutions were incorrectly prepared. High readings usually mean that previous irrigations have not been of great enough volume to leach salts out of the pot, or that fertilizer stocks were made too concentrated.

48

Low levels of nitrogen induce lower leaf senescence. To combat this problem, urea formaldehyde top dressing at 1 teaspoon per 6-in. pot about one to two weeks after emergence is recommended (Miller 1985). This procedure is highly effective in regions where prolonged periods of dark, cold weather can occur during forcing. In the Sunbelt, urea formaldehyde is not needed. This is due to the high rate of water loss by the plants caused by high light, low humidity, and large greenhouse ventilation rates. Because of the need for frequent watering (and thus fertilization) in the Sunbelt, optimum levels of nutrients should always be available. In fact, one crop experienced severe damage after application of urea formaldehyde due to rapid ammonia volatilization caused by warm soil temperatures.

Phosphorus is an essential element, and can be supplied by pre-plant incorporation of a phosphorus-containing complete fertilizer, or by irrigating with soluble phosphorus (up to 50 ppm) during forcing. Where irrigation water is alkaline, phosphoric acid may be used to lower irrigation water pH. For example, at the University of Arizona about 45 ppm phosphorus comes from water acidification with phosphoric acid. We had four excellent lily crops with this method.

Trace elements are a poorly understood component of lily nutrition. With growing media containing 20–35% loam, trace element deficiencies are rare. With soil-less media, occasional applications of soluble trace elements or a pre-plant trace element incorporation (Table 7) is recommended.

Carbon Dioxide Enrichment

Since much of their growth occurs in the winter and early spring when greenhouses are tightly closed, it would seem that lilies would be an ideal crop for carbon dioxide enrichment in northern areas. Most studies, however, indicate that lilies do not respond favorably to CO_2 enrichment. In work at Minnesota (Wilkins et al. 1968), lilies given supplemental CO_2 were taller, but flowered at the same time as controls without an increase in flower count or overall plant quality. Thus, there is no benefit to CO_2 supplementation for Easter lilies. There is no work on CO_2 for hybrid lilies, but it is likely they would show similar responses as Easter lilies.

Height Control

For most pot plants, an aesthetic ratio of plant height to pot diameter is 2.6:1 (Sachs et al. 1976). Thus, for a 6-in. pot, the "optimum" aesthetic height (including the pot) for a lily is 15.6 in. Throw the aesthetic ratio out the door, however, when you are marketing your plants. Chain store outlets are increasingly concerned about exact specifications for finished plants. The best height for your plants is the height your customer wants them.

Height control is critical in Easter lilies because of increased market demand for shorter, more compact plants. Also, trucking costs are lower on a unit basis if shorter plants are grown, i.e., more boxes of 18-in. tall plants can fit into a truck than boxes filled with 27-in. tall plants.

Factors affecting finished plant height are given in Table 9. Height varies among lily cultivars, with 'Ace' generally being taller than 'Nellie White'. One of the most common causes of excessively tall lilies is low light levels in the greenhouse resulting in long internodes and stretched plants (Post 1941; Kiplinger 1953; Kohl and Nelson 1963). Plants grown under reduced light also have spindly stems, thinner leaves (Einert and Box 1967), and lower levels of leaf and flower bud carbohydrates (Miller and Langhans 1989b). Figure 13 (color plate) shows typical responses to low greenhouse light.

Table 9. Factors affecting final plant height of Easter lilies.

1. Long days increase plant height, short days decrease height.
2. Low irradiance (greenhouse light intensity) increases plant height.
3. Low fertilizer levels, especially nitrogen, increase lily height.
4. Increased flower numbers increase plant height.
5. Higher forcing temperatures cause taller lilies.
6. Close spacing (pot-to-pot) increases plant height.

PHOTOPERIOD

Lilies elongate under "long day" conditions (Smith and Langhans 1962b). Long days (16 hr.) for 10-day periods resulted in a 19–21% height increase in lilies, relative to plants in the natural daylengths of January and February (Table 10). However, the natural daylength in February, March, and April is long enough to cause additional stem elongation relative to artificial 8-hr. short days. Short days (8 hr.) for the entire forcing period resulted in a 29% height reduction as compared to plants grown under prevailing natural daylengths (Table 11). Even if used for relatively short specific periods in the crop cycle, short

Table 10. Effect of long days (16 hours) for 10-day periods on height and bud count in 'Nellie White' Easter lilies (Heins et al. 1982b).

Days after emergence, plants given long days	Bud count	Height (in.)	Percent height increase
Natural daylength (no LD)	5.8	12.6	—
0–10	6.1	15.0	19
10–20	6.0	15.4	22
15–25	6.4	15.4	22
20–30	6.4	15.7	25
25–35	5.8	15.0	19
30–40	6.7	15.4	22
40 long days	5.8	15.4	22

51

days significantly reduce plant height without a delay in flowering (Table 11).

Lilies usually double in height from the visible bud stage to flowering (Heins et al. 1982a). This phenomenon likely has several contributing factors, including the presence of flower buds and a better developed root system, warmer prevailing plant temperatures due to seasonally increasing light levels, and the seasonal increase in daylength. All of this height increase is due to *internode elongation*, and not to an increase in leaf number. Since half of the plant height is determined in this relatively brief period, short days can be expected to lead to shorter lilies. In fact, short days applied between visible bud and flowering reduced plant height by 20% in both 'Ace' and 'Nellie White' (Heins et al. 1982b) (Table 11).

To summarize, if automatic black cloth is available, short days should be considered for height control, especially later in the crop when total available light is increasing. This point is important, as short days cause a lower dry weight percentage as compared to long days (Kohl and Nelson 1963). This is because less time is allowed for photosynthesis. Plants with less dry weight are usually considered to be of lower quality, with possibly reduced post-production quality.

Another reason for tall plants is greenhouse temperature. Warmer day temperatures (positive DIFs)

Table 11. Effects of short days (8 hr.) for different growth stages on height and bud count in 'Ace' and 'Nellie White' lilies (Heins et al. 1982b).

Period plants were given short days	Bud count	Plant height (in.)	Percent height reduction	Days from emergence to flowering
Natural days (no SD)	4.4	16.1	0	99
Emergence to flowering	3.0	11.3	29	99
Bud initiation to flowering	4.4	13.0	19	95
Visible bud to flowering	3.4	12.8	20	99

lead to taller lilies (Smith and Langhans 1962a; Erwin et al. 1987, 1988, 1989). Where high temperatures are necessary late in the crop cycle for forcing slower lilies, additional stretch occurs.

As flower number increases, plant height also increases, with most of the additional height coming from extra elongation in the upper one-fourth of the stem.

TEMPERATURE MANIPULATION

Most plants respond to thermoperiodism, or the alteration of day and night greenhouse temperatures. In the 1940s at Cal Tech, Dr. Frits Went conducted a series of investigations that demonstrated more vigorous plant growth when day temperatures were greater then night temperatures. Most of his research was conducted on tomato and chile pepper. This work formed the basis for the common practice of maintaining night greenhouse temperatures lower than daily temperatures.

Recent research has taken advantage of Went's concepts, and has demonstrated that a substantial level of floricultural crop height control is possible by using higher night than day temperatures. This phenomenon, coined DIF (difference between day and night temperature), is very effective for Easter lilies, and has been reported extensively in the trade literature (Erwin et al. 1987, 1988; Heins et al. 1987). Essentially, growing lilies under warmer night temperatures than day temperatures results in stunting of plant growth, and reduced final plant height. Greater height restriction is seen with a greater difference between day and night temperature, i.e., for a given day temperature the warmer the night, the shorter the plants. This is shown in Figure 14, where final lily plant height is plotted against the difference in air temperature (DT-NT).

In terms of plant development, however, it has been established that, within most commercial situations, many plants respond to an average of day and night temperature (Miller and Langhans 1985; Karlsson et al.

53

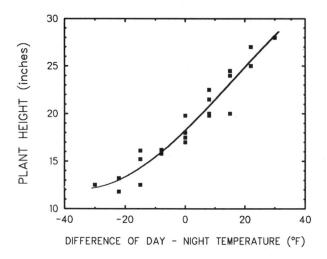

Figure 14. Effect of day-night temperatures (DIF) on height in Easter lilies.

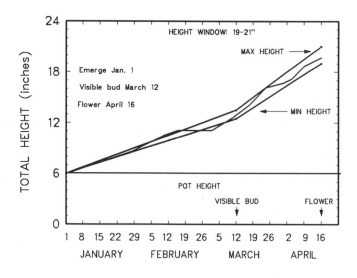

Figure 15. Example of a "graphical track" window for Easter lilies.

54

1988). With Easter lilies, similar rates of leaf unfolding occurs with an 80°/60°F (day/night, 12 hr. each) regime as with a 60°/80°F regime, since each averages 70°F. This is advantageous because it allows the selection of a range of day/night temperature differentials which should result in variable height reduction, but all with the same developmental rate. These factors have been integrated into useful "graphical tracking" procedures that allow the grower to monitor more closely the development of their crop. The graphical tracking concept is reviewed below.

A typical graphical track for an Easter lily crop is given in Figure 15. There are a few simple steps that must be followed to establish a graph for your operation, and are given in Table 12.

Table 12. Procedure for establishing a height tracking window.

1. Establish the desired final height. This might be 19–22 in. including the pot. Subtracting 6 in. for the pot gives 13–16 in. of actual plant height.
2. Establish the desired visible bud date. Usually figure five to six weeks before Easter.
3. On a piece of graph paper, plot time along the bottom, and height along the left side (see Fig. 13).
4. Draw a line at 6 in. to account for the pot. Mark the maximum (22 in.) and minimum (19 in.) heights at flowering.
5. Calculate the required visible bud height, on the rule of thumb that the plant doubles in height from VB to flowering. Thus, half of the final 13–16 in. plant height is 6.5–8 in. at VB. Adding 6 in. for the pot gives VB heights of 12.5–14 in. to be added to the graph.
6. Connect the maximum flowering and VB heights, and the minimum heights. This gives the height window for the period of VB to flowering. The VB points are extended back to the 6 in. (zero plant height) line at emergence, giving a window for the whole crop.
7. Remember that only the plant doubles in height from VB to flowering, *not* the plant plus pot!

MAKING AND USING THE GRAPHICAL TRACKING WINDOW

With the window established, the optimum combination of controlled leaf unfolding and height control can be determined after flower bud initiation. The concept of leaf unfolding is identical to that described in the scheduling section. Height control is due to the uniform response of plants to average temperatures. Work at Michigan State University (Karlsson et al. 1988) has led to the development of the graph in Figure 16. This graph is a plot of leaf unfolding as affected by day and night temperatures at a daylength of 10 hr. Knowing the required leaf unfolding rate (as determined by leaf counts), a range of day/night combinations are possible that give the same daily rate of leaf unfolding. The temperature ranges are also the key to height control: the greater the night temperature relative to the day temperature, the lower the stem elongation rate. Thus, if 1.6 leaves needed to be unfolded each day, a day/night temperature of 70°/61°F

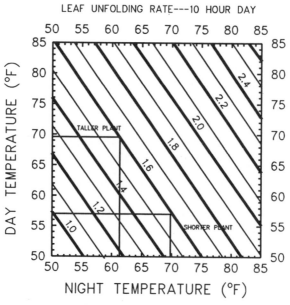

Figure 16. Isopleth plot of leaf unfolding at a 10-hr. daylength.

could be selected. Because of the higher day temperature, this combination will cause the stem to elongate. On the other hand, a 57°/70°F day/night temperature provides the same average temperature and the same rate of leaf unfolding, but inhibits stem elongation relative to 70°/60°F. Thus, a range of day/night temperature combinations may be chosen that give the same rate of leaf unfolding, but with different rates of stem elongation. By measuring a group of plants every couple of days, plotting the average height and consulting your individually constructed tracking chart (e.g., Fig. 15), leaves can be unfolded at the needed rate while keeping plants within the required height window.

Although not fully investigated, it should be assumed that higher night temperatures than day will cause a reduction in the carbohydrate status of the plant. Plants with high levels of carbohydrate in the leaves, stems, and flowers usually have better post-production performance. Reversed night temperatures (negative DIFs) cause a reduction in plant dry matter, and a reduction in percentage plant dry weight in lilies (Zieslin and Tsujita 1988). In poinsettia, increases in night temperature from 48° to 63°F (8.9°–17.2°C) reduced total leaf carbohydrate by 41% (Senecal et al. 1989). 'Nellie White' lilies grown at Purdue University with a 10°F negative DIF (60°/70°F, day/night) had 25% fewer leaf carbohydrates than control plants grown at a 10-degree positive DIF (70°/60°F) (W. B. Miller and P. A. Hammer, unpublished data). Also, the use of warmer night temperatures for Easter lilies can cause excessive downward curling of foliage and yellowing of lower leaves (Erwin et al. 1987, 1988, 1989). Lily leaf yellowing is associated with reduced leaf carbohydrate (Jiao et al. 1986; W. B. Miller and D. A. Bailey, unpublished data). Growers should be aware of the potential post-production problems when very large night to day temperature differentials are used. It is essential that growers maintain high standards of production, and be aware of implications of management practices which reduce final plant quality.

Growers should first experiment on a small scale with reversed temperatures for height control. Temperature reversal is a good tool for lily height control, but should not be looked upon as a way of eliminating the need for other crop production skills.

SPACING PRACTICES

Plants that are spaced close together show increased stem elongation or "stretching." This can be a serious problem in the few weeks after flower bud initiation before plants are moved to final spacing. Final spacing depends on many market and economic factors, but 2.5 pots per square ft. (about 8 × 7 in.) is a commonly used rule. Plants must be spaced promptly after flower bud initiation for highest final plant quality. For better uniformity, some growers move the tallest plants to the edge of the bench, and place the shortest in the center of the bench, producing a "dish" of plant height when viewed from the end of the bench. This practice tends to stretch the shorter plants in the center and inhibit elongation of the already tall plants on the edge. Some growers, however, produce the entire crop at nearly pot-to-pot spacing, usually with high applications of growth regulators (see the "Growth Regulators" section). Yellowing and dieback of lower leaves is usually seen with this method of forcing.

MECHANICAL STRESS AND ETHYLENE

Scientists have long known that plants which are mechanically stressed are shorter and stouter that non-stressed plants. In the early 1970s, researchers at U.C. Davis showed that shaking trees for 15 seconds per day significantly reduced elongation (Neel and Harris 1971), and in 1975 Japanese scientists (Hiraki and Ota 1975) confirmed this with Easter lily. Earlier reports (in Japanese) also exist reporting that mechanical stress reduces final height in Easter and Oriental hybrid lilies (Matsukawa and Kashiwaga 1971). Turgeon and Webb (1971) found that the simple act of measuring leaf growth of cucumber reduced the growth of the leaves they were measuring! Keep this phenomenon in mind when measuring lilies for graphical tracking. Probably, plants being graphically tracked grow just a little less than the rest of the crop due to the regular mechanical stress involved in measuring them. Plants should be disturbed as little as possible during measurement.

Figure 17 (color plate) shows results of an experiment where 'Nellie White' plants were mechanically stressed by running a finger around the leaves of the plant 10 times once each day. Growth has been reduced and the leaves are epinastic. The Japanese researchers showed that increased ethylene production caused the growth reduction. Flowering in the mechanically stressed plants in Figure 17 was delayed by about two weeks.

Ethephon (Florel™ or Ethrel™) releases the plant growth hormone ethylene when it is sprayed onto plants. While moderate levels of ethephon cause flower abortion and blast in lilies (see "Physiological Disorders" section), very low concentrations (less than 100 ppm) can effectively reduce plant height without flower injury. Table 13 shows height reduction and flower abortion by ethephon at several rates. It is clear that great care must be taken in

Table 13. Effect of ethephon on height control and flower abortion in Easter lily.

Ethephon (ppm)	Final plant height (in.)	Aborted buds (%)
0	11.6	0
100	10.3	0
300	9.8	30
500	9.1	13
400	9.1	50
500	9.3	87

mixing and applying ethephon for height control in Easter lilies. Only growers with accurate measuring equipment and well-maintained sprayers should try this means of height control, and only on a trial basis.

GROWTH REGULATORS

Chemical growth regulation of Easter lilies has been used for about 30 years. Stuart et al. (1961) reported that Phosphon-D™, at 2.25 grams active ingredient per pot, reduced 'Georgia' lily height by about 30%. We are fortunate that more effective chemicals have been developed, because this rate comes to nearly 500 pounds for a crop of 100,000 lilies!

A-REST™

In the early 1970s, ancymidol (A-Rest™) became available for commercial use. While expensive, A-Rest™ was a boon to lily forcing, as it provided reliable height control without undue side effects. Both spray and drench applications are effective for height control under a wide range of environmental conditions. Currently, A-Rest™ is the only effective material registered for use on Easter lilies. Table 14 gives guidelines for preparing A-Rest™ solutions for spray or drench applications. Usually, the first A-Rest™ application is made prior to the time shoots are 3 in. tall, with additional applications later on as necessary.

Only through grower experience can optimum levels of A-Rest™ be determined. In areas where crops are usually tall, two or three A-Rest™ drenches totaling up to 1 mg are necessary. Other growers prefer multiple sprays (25–50 ppm) resulting in small increments of height control over a longer time period. Growing media with a significant bark percentage will adsorb A-Rest™ and make it unavailable for uptake by the plant. For this reason, growers should not use A-Rest™ drenches if growing in bark media.

Bulb dips into solutions of A-Rest™ are also effective in reducing final plant height (Lewis and Lewis 1982). Table 15 shows that bulb quick dips up to 264 ppm (full strength A-Rest™) progressively reduce plant height, but also increase forcing time relative to the controls. Other work has shown that 30-min. dips in the range of 0 to 33 ppm A-Rest™ also give effective control (Larson and Thorne 1988). There has rarely been a decrease in flower number with dips, and no increase in root rot has occurred.

All of the research with bulb dips has shown yearly variability in effectiveness and response. This could be due to physiological differences in the bulbs, in the amount of growth regulator-absorbing soil on each individual bulb, or other factors. The technique is not commercially recommended on a large scale, but growers are encouraged to try small, experimental plots under their own conditions.

able 14. Guidelines for mixing A-Rest™ spray and drench solutions for Easter lilies.

-Rest™, 0.0264% active ingredient, or, 250 mg a.i. per quart.

pray	Spray solution	fl oz. A-Rest™/gal. of final solution	qt. A-Rest™/100 gal. final solution	ml A-Rest™/liter final solution
qt./	25 ppm	12.1	37.8	99.2
)0 sq. ft.)	33 ppm	16.0	50.0	130.9
	50 ppm	24.2	75.6	189.3

rench	Dose (mg/pot)	ppm	fl oz. A-Rest™/gal. of final solution	ml A-Rest™/liter of final solution	qt. A-Rest™/10 gal. (with 1:100 injection)
fl oz.	0.10	0.6	0.27	2.1	8.5
er pot)	0.25	1.4	0.68	5.3	21.2
	0.50	2.8	1.36	10.6	42.5

uidelines are provided for informational purposes only. No endorsement is intended for oducts mentioned, nor is criticism meant for products not mentioned. Before purchasing and ;ing any agricultural chemical, you, as the user, must check all labels for registered use, rates, and •plication frequency. It is illegal to use any chemical in a manner inconsistent with its labeling.

Table 15. Effects of a 2-second bulb quick dip into A-Rest™ solutions before or after 6 weeks of cooling. Excess solution allowed to drain, then planted. (Note: 264 ppm is full strength A-Rest™.) All plants averaged 5.7 flowers.

Treatment	Final height (in.)	Days to flower
Control	18.7	139
Pre-cool bulb dips		
25 ppm	16.3	133
50 ppm	14.3	137
100 ppm	12.6	140
200 ppm	12.0	148
264 ppm	10.9	149
Post-cool bulb dips		
25 ppm	18.0	135
50 ppm	17.2	140
100 ppm	16.5	142
200 ppm	11.5	143
264 ppm	11.7	160

TRIAZOLES (SUMAGIC™)

Recent developments in triazole chemistry has led to numerous new compounds useful for Easter lily height control. Interestingly, triazoles were originally developed as fungicides, but show powerful plant growth regulating properties as well (Wulster et al. 1987). Like many other floricultural growth regulators, they inhibit gibberellin synthesis, and lead to plants with reduced internode lengths. The most effective of these compounds for Easter lilies is *uniconazole* (XE-1019) or Sumagic™, made by Valent, USA. Barring unforeseen problems, Sumagic™ should be available in the United States for the 1992 forcing season.

I estimate that Sumagic™ is about 5 to 10 times more effective than A-Rest™ on Easter lilies. Because of this extremely high activity, it is important for growers to review and upgrade spray procedures. Sumagic™ is translocated in the xylem, with very little phloem mobility. This raises a new concern because the site of application on the plant has a large influence on the efficacy of the chemical. For any given dose, maximal growth reduction occurs from root uptake, stem uptake, then leaf uptake. This is a fundamentally different situation than with B-Nine™ or Cycocel™ with mums or poinsettias, where sprays to runoff are standard procedure. With Sumagic™, a given spray dose will have varying effects depending on the volume with which it is applied. Higher volumes cause more to wash into the soil, causing more root uptake, with greater plant stunting.

Starting ranges for Sumagic™ are 10–30 ppm spray applications, with an application volume of 2 qt. per 100 square ft. of bench area. A suggested starting range for Sumagic™ soil drenches is 0.05–0.15 mg a.i. per pot. Mixing guidelines are given in Table 16. Bark growing media have been reported to adsorb Sumagic™ as well, so growers using bark media are advised to rely on Sumagic™ sprays.

Table 16. Guidelines for mixing Sumagic™ spray and drench solutions for Easter lilies.

Sumagic™, 500 ppm active ingredient.

Spray	Spray solution	fl oz. Sumagic™/ gal. final solution	qt. Sumagic™/100 gal. final solution	ml Sumagic™/liter final solution
2 qt./	10 ppm	2.6	8.0	20
100 sq. ft.)	20 ppm	5.2	16.0	40
	30 ppm	7.8	24.0	60

Drench	Dose (mg/pot)	ppm	qt. Sumagic™/10 gal. (with 1:100 injection)
6 fl oz.	0.05	0.28	2.24
per pot)	0.10	0.56	4.48
	0.15	0.84	6.72

Guidelines are provided for informational purposes only. No endorsement is intended for products mentioned, nor is criticism meant for products not mentioned. Before purchasing and using any agricultural chemical, you, as the user, must check all labels for registered use, rates, and application frequency. It is illegal to use any chemical in a manner inconsistent with its labeling.

It should be obvious that since Sumagic™ is very effective, one should be cautious when first working with it. Set up small test plots: do not treat the whole crop the first time! *Measure* the height of your crops; keep track of the height on a semi-weekly basis to become more familiar with the growth pattern of the crop. If the crop is already too tall, no chemical will shorten it.

Wulster et al. (1987) found several triazole fungicides (propiconazol [Banner™], triadimefon [Bayleton™], and Mobay RSW0411) to be effective in reducing lily plant height, either as bulb dips or soil drenches. The rates which caused excessive height control were higher than those required for disease control. Integrated disease and height control with a single chemical may be possible, since the rates necessary for disease control do not cause excessive plant stunting. Additional research is required to fully implement this principle, and new ways to reduce chemical applications to the crop are welcome. It also points out the increasing number of options and technical aspects of the floriculture industry.

Much work has indicated that Bonzi™ is effective on Easter lilies, although massive doses (up to 5.0 mg a.i. per pot) are required for adequate height control (Gianfagna and Wulster 1986; Wilfret 1987). These rates are 10 times more than necessary with A-Rest™, and about 30 to 40 times those needed with Sumagic™. Clearly, Bonzi™ should not be used on Easter or hybrid lilies, and a recent report (Tayama 1990) recommending Bonzi™ drenches in the range of 0.125 to 0.5 mg a.i. per pot should be ignored.

GIBBERELLIN

Research was conducted in the early 1970s to see if gibberellic acid (GA) could substitute for some or all of the vernalization treatment. While this goal was not met, several other observations on Easter lily response to GA were made. GA applied prior to flower bud initiation (as a 1000-ppm soil drench) tended to reduce flower formation, and caused additional flower abortion later in forcing (De Hertogh and Blakely 1972). GA_{4+7} was more detrimental then GA_3. These rates also tended to reduce stem thickness, and increased height somewhat.

These experiments have relevance today. With the increasingly powerful triazole growth regulators being available, there may be a need to use GA to rescue plants from growth regulator overdoses. Based on the earlier work, GA_{4+7} would be the most effective GA to use. A starting range might be 100–200 ppm GA_{4+7}. Very large positive DIFs (day temperature 10° to 20°F higher than night temperature) might also be effective in forcing growth regulator retarded plants to elongate. The best policy will be to calculate carefully the growth regulator needed, and apply as described above. These is no inherent reason that overdoses should occur with proper care.

Post-production Handling and Physiology

PACKING AND SHIPPING

Generally, most lilies are sleeved and placed in boxes for shipment to market. Corrugated cardboard boxes are used. Polyethylene box liners were recently shown to reduce moisture loss from plants, but had no effect on leaf chlorosis or floral longevity (Prince and Cunningham 1989). However, given the potential for *Botrytis* infection from condensation inside the boxes, poly liners are not a good idea, and should not be used.

The optimum sleeving and boxing time in the greenhouse is one to three days before the first flower opens. With this schedule and a relatively short shipping distance, plants open their first flower the day of unpacking at the point of sale. This minimizes bruising of open flowers during transit, and provides optimum consumer enjoyment. Pollen causes yellow staining of the corolla, so pollen removal is important if plants must be shipped with open flowers. It is best to ship before flowers open. Pollen removal has no effect on longevity of individual flowers (Tsukushi 1970).

COLD STORAGE OF BUDDED PLANTS

Because of the very narrow market window, lilies are one of the most difficult crops to bring into flower, pack, ship, and deliver to the market. And because of the nature of the bulb and the numerous factors affecting vernalization, there is a range of flowering dates within any population of bulbs. This range of optimum harvest dates is wider than for most other crops that are scheduled by, for example, photoperiod. The result is that, even with the crop perfectly timed, 5–15% of the crop will come into flower several days earlier than the crop average. If no market exists directly at the time, these plants (at or before the "puffy bud stage") can be placed in a dark cooler at 34°–40°F (1.1°–4.4°C). If lights are left on in the cooler, stretching will occur. The low temperature reduces the rate of flower development and opening, and thus allows growers to select advanced plants and hold them prior to shipping or sale. One week or less of storage has little or no adverse effect on longevity after storage. With three weeks of storage, many buds will fail to open properly, and quality is greatly reduced.

Some growers deliberately schedule their lilies several days early to reduce the chance of missing Easter. In reality, this is a poor practice because the basic frenzy of activity of getting the crop shipped is merely moved ahead by a few days, and the logistics of getting the major portion of the crop in and out of the cooler are problematic.

Five major problems can develop with prolonged cold storage: bud abortion (blast), foliar chlorosis, reduced flower longevity, *Botrytis* infection, and physiological wilt after removal from the cooler. To control *Botrytis*, benomyl (Benlate™ 50WP) may be sprayed to runoff (0.75 oz. per 10 gal.) before plants are put in the cooler. Allow the solution to dry before moving into the cooler. Plants should never be stored in plastic sleeves while in the cooler: moisture condensation on leaves and flowers will occur, greatly increasing the danger of *Botrytis*. Paper sleeves reduce this danger by absorbing water, but can deteriorate due to moisture in the cooler. If sleeves must be used in the cooler, paper is the best choice.

Individual flowers of cold-stored plants do not persist as long as flowers of non-stored plants. 'Nellie White' flowers lasted 7.3 days with no storage, and only 4.6 days with two weeks of storage at 33°–43°F (Staby and Erwin 1977). In another study, when 'Nellie White' plants were stored in the puffy bud stage for four weeks their floral longevity was reduced by 27% (Prince et al. 1987).

Foliar chlorosis begins with lower leaves, and is a problem that rapidly develops after removal from the cooler. 'Nellie White' lilies stored for four weeks at 36°F (2.2°C) developed 88% leaf chlorosis in the interior environment (Prince et al. 1987). Floral longevity was decreased 27%, and bud blast increased as cold storage increased (Table 17). Obviously, the goal for best consumer acceptance, satisfaction, and future sales is proper timing so than minimal or no storage is necessary.

Application of silver thiosulfate (STS) reduces storage-induced flower bud abortion, but does not reduce

Table 17. **Effect of length of 36°F (2°C) storage on bud blast, foliar chlorosis, and floral longevity of 'Nellie White' lilies (Prince et al. 1987).**

Weeks of storage	Aborted buds (%)	Chlorotic foliage (%)	Average flower longevity (days)
0	0	20	8.3
1	4	37	8.3
2	30	50	7.3
3	23	66	6.3
4	39	88	6.1

the foliar chlorosis that develops after storage. STS improved floral longevity by only 0.4 day (with a total individual flower life of nine days) (Prince et al. 1987), which is insignificant from the consumer's point of view. Thus, while reduction of ethylene action appears to be an important factor in preventing some lily post-production disorders, other factors are involved.

Since dark-stored lilies no longer photosynthesize, leaf senescence and reduced flower longevity may be due to carbohydrate depletion. Respiration, a carbohydrate-consuming process, continues in darkness, and increases with higher temperature. Thus, carbohydrate depletion will be greater at higher temperatures. This is clearly shown in Figure 18. 'Nellie White' plants at the puffy bud stage were sleeved and placed in a cooler at 40°F for up to three weeks. Other plants were sleeved and placed in shipping boxes at 70°F for up to six days. Figure 18 indicates that 70°F dark storage reduced leaf carbo-

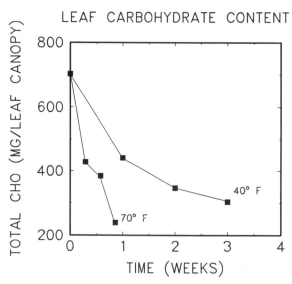

Figure 18. Effect of 0–6 days of 70°F dark storage or 0–3 weeks of 40°F dark storage on total carbohydrates in 'Nellie White' Easter lily leaves (W. B. Miller, unpublished data).

hydrate level by 67% in only six days. Storage at 40°F reduced leaf carbohydrate levels by 57%, but it took three weeks.

In the absence of new carbohydrate from photosynthesis, plants are dependent upon food materials stored in the leaves, stems, flowers, or bulbs for continued respiration and maintenance. Research (Miller and Langhans 1989b) showed that long periods (at least four weeks) of "carbohydrate stress" conditions are required before the bulb begins to "give up" additional food reserves to the shoot. Carbohydrates are probably being transported from leaves to the flower buds, accounting for yellow basal leaves after long storage periods. Over time, the foliage cannot satisfy the carbohydrate demands of the flowers, and flowers tend to abort with very long storage periods. Additional research on these questions is needed to improve commercial recommendations and our understanding of these processes.

Finally, it should be emphasized that lilies should not be removed from the cooler and placed directly into a warm, sunny greenhouse. The cold soil mass and root system prevent water uptake to meet the needs of the warming shoot system. Physiological wilt and bud sunburn can easily result. The best solution is to remove plants in the evening so that plants can warm in the dark in the greenhouse.

FERTILIZATION AND POST-PRODUCTION QUALITY

Recently, researchers have investigated the effects of fertilizer termination of lily post-production performance. Termination of fertilizer at visible bud, or at two weeks after visible bud, caused increased lower leaf chlorosis relative to plants that were fertilized until harvest (Prince and Cunningham 1989). In this experiment, all plants were held at 36°F (2.2°C) for three weeks prior to consumer evaluation. Thus, unlike poinsettia and chrysanthemum, where post-production quality is enhanced by reducing fertilizer in the final stages of forcing, lilies should be fertilized nearly up to the time of harvest. Because of generally poor watering practices in the average retail outlet and the potential for drying out, it is probably best to have lily soil depleted of most fertilizer salts before shipping. Clear water irrigations in the last week of forcing should accomplish this.

EFFECT OF PRODUCTION ENVIRONMENT AND GROWTH REGULATORS ON POST-PRODUCTION QUALITY

In areas with extremely high greenhouse light levels such as the Southwest and Southeast, 30% shading during forcing does not affect foliar senescence (during actual forcing or during the post-harvest evaluation). The growth regulator uniconazole (Sumagic™), when used at rates above 10 ppm, did, however, increase leaf senescence during forcing and during the post-production phase (Table 18).

Table 18. **Effects of Sumagic™ (uniconazole) sprays on 'Nellie White' plant height and leaf senescence before and during 2–3 weeks of post-production evaluation (PPE) (W. B. Miller and D. A. Bailey, unpublished data).**

Sumagic spray rate (ppm)	Number of sprays	Leaves senescent at flowering (%)	Leaves senescing during PPE (%)	Leaves senescent at end of PPE (%)
Control	1	4	9	13
5	1	4	8	12
10	1	7	14	21
15	1	10	15	25
20	1	13	26	39
5	2	7	11	18
10	2	12	18	30
15	2	19	38	57

A new post-production disorder has appeared with the advent of using reversed temperatures (DIFs) for height control. Negative DIFs (nights warmer than days, and causing shorter plants) induce potentially severe leaf epinasty and leaf chlorosis. The symptoms disappear after one to two weeks of "normal" greenhouse temperatures. It is thus important to avoid using strong DIF temperatures in the final two weeks of forcing to give the plants time to regain their normal and desirable leaf orientation and color.

EFFECT OF CONSUMER ENVIRONMENT

No specific studies of the effect of the consumer environment (temperature, relative humidity, etc.) have been conducted, and likely are not practical nor especially useful. General recommendations to be given consumers would be to place lilies in a bright sunny location that does not get above 75°F (24°C). Plants should be watered thoroughly every two to four days, but the soil should not be kept wet. With proper care, each flower should last five to eight days, although the first flowers tend to last a day or two longer than later-opening flowers. On the average plant, the entire inflorescence should be attractive for 15 to 20 days. Flowers should be removed as they senesce.

Physiological Disorders of Easter Lilies

A physiological disorder is one that is not disease- or insect-caused. Many of these problems have no clear, easy explanation or solution.

Leaf scorch. This disorder appears as sickle-shaped lesions that form near the leaf tip (Fig. 19, color plate). The lesions appear rapidly, progressing from slightly depressed areas on the upper leaf surface to brown necrotic lesions within a day or two. The boundary of necrotic and healthy tissue is not sharply defined, i.e., there is a region of chlorotic tissue between them (Fig. 20, color plate). The disorder is nutritional, caused primarily by fluoride (Marousky and Woltz 1977). Common fluoride sources are superphosphate fertilizer, perlite, and fluoridated municipal water. 'Nellie White' is more resistant to leaf scorch than 'Ace', while 'Croft', an old cultivar, was devastated by leaf scorch. Susceptibility to scorch has a genetic component (Roberts and Moeller 1979), and newer cultivars should be evaluated for scorch resistance prior to increase.

Fortunately, leaf scorch is an easily controlled problem. The cultivar 'Nellie White' is very resistant to scorch, and with higher soil pH less injury is seen. See the discussion of chemical characteristics in the "Growing Medium" section and the "Nutrition and Fertilization" section.

A second type of leaf scorch, caused by boron toxicity, also occurs (Fig. 20). This scorch is distinguishable from fluoride scorch by the fact that the necrotic tissue at the leaf tip are sharply delineated from healthy tissue, without a chlorotic region. This type of scorch can occur on any lily cultivar. The likely source of boron is irrigation water in localized regions of the country. Growers in high boron areas should be aware of this problem.

Lower leaf yellowing and senescence. This disorder can be due to many factors, and causes severe quality losses if not controlled (Fig. 21, color plate). Some of the factors involved in leaf senescence follow:

1. Low nitrogen fertilization causes leaf loss. During periods of prolonged dark, cloudy weather, plants do not transpire very much, and it is difficult to add sufficient nitrogen through normal liquid fertilizer injection. A top dressing of 1 teaspoon urea formaldehyde per pot will add extra nitrogen to the plant, and will help reduce leaf loss. Additional information can be found in the "Nutrition and Fertilization" section.

2. Leaf senescence has also been linked to phosphorous (P) nutrition with an interesting interaction with growth regulators and leaf carbohydrate. Tsujita et al. (1978, 1979) found that A-Rest™ drenches in commercially useful ranges (0–0.5 mg/pot drench) progressively increase lower leaf senescence. Spray applications of A-Rest™ (up to the equivalent of 0.5 mg/pot) can also cause leaf senescence, but the effect is not as severe as with drenches. Low P nutrition worsens the A-Rest™ effect. Higher rates of P nutrition increase leaf P, and reduce A-Rest™-induced leaf senescence. Thus, maintenance of optimum P levels will help combat lower leaf senescence.

3. Loss of lower leaves is also highly symptomatic of root rot. A preventative fungicidal program should help eliminate this problem. The possibility that root rot was a factor in the high A-Rest™ treated plants (see above) was discounted (Tsujita et al. 1979). Lilies are, however, extremely sensitive to over-watering, and plants growing in soggy soils are almost certainly going to exhibit lower leaf loss. This may be a real factor in growth regulator-induced leaf senescence. Since the growth regulator reduces plant size, transpiration is reduced, and plants will tend to be over-watered with the danger of increased leaf loss.

4. Leaf senescence was correlated with reduced levels of leaf sugar and starch (Jiao et al. 1986; Miller and Bailey unpublished data). The triazole growth regulators, most notably uniconazole (Sumagic™) can cause lower leaf carbohydrates and lower leaf yellowing in the greenhouse and post-production phases, as discussed in that section (Table 18). These findings do not mean that growth regulators should be discarded from the arsenal of tools the grower has to produce a high quality lily crop; but growers must always be concerned with quality, and be aware of the side effects of a given treatment.

Close plant spacing will shade lower leaves, reduce leaf sugars, reduce total plant transpiration, and lead to a greater average water content of the pot, all leading to more leaf yellowing. Although no replicated studies are available, grower experiences indicate the stress of high temperature forcing exacerbates any leaf yellowing present. While cultural recommendations to combat lower leaf senescence are common, little is known about its physiological origin. The available research does little to solve the problem. For example, while extra nitrogen tends to reduce leaf scorch, no correlation exists between foliar nitrogen level and lower leaf senescence (Prince and Cunningham 1989). Thus, lower leaf senescence is not simply nitrogen deficiency. Clearly, leaf senescence is a complicated disorder caused by many factors, acting singly or in combination.

Bud abortion. While all types of bud death (including bud "blast," see below) during development are technically bud "abortion," growers usually reserve the term bud abortion to describe bud death at a very early stage, as in Figure 22 (color plate). While many research papers have been published on bud abortion or bud blast, a distinction is rarely made between the two. This makes comparison of treatments which induce one or the other of these problems difficult. My research has indicated that heavy (50% or more) shading early in the growth cycle (emergence to flower bud initiation) causes a significant increase (one or more buds per plant) in abortion with 'Nellie White'. Given the sensitivity of other bulb crops to ethylene, it seems likely that ethylene could also be involved with this disorder. Since there is no information available on ethylene and flower bud abortion, more research is needed to determine the ultimate cause of this important physiological disorder.

Bud blasting (Fig. 23, color plate). From a scientific standpoint, a blasted bud is an aborted bud. Commercially, however, a blasted bud is one that ceased development after it was relatively large, perhaps 0.25 in. or more. Based on early work with 'Croft', reduced leaf and plant carbohydrate is commonly thought to be the major cause of lily bud blast (Post 1941; Mastalerz 1965). However, numerous studies with 'Nellie White' have shown that growing plants under shade treatments that would be expected to reduce plant carbohydrate level usually causes very little bud blast. Another factor influencing bud blast, ethylene, is little appreciated by growers. Ethylene at 1 ppm for 10 hr. is able to induce blasting of intact, 2-in. long buds (Rhoads et al. 1973). Larger buds were unaffected. Much of the bud blast seen in commercial greenhouses may be due to ethylene accumulated within the greenhouse atmosphere from physical or biological sources, rather than to low light levels per se. Conditions favoring "carbohydrate depletion" (cold, dark days and nights with the greenhouse tightly closed and heaters running all night) also are conditions when ethylene could accumulate. The lower limit of ethylene injury to lilies is not known, but is likely much less than 1 ppm overnight. A simple test for ethylene contamination is to keep a tomato plant in the greenhouse. If ethylene is present, the leaves and petioles will curl downwards (epinasty). Growers are advised to be aware of ethylene pollution in their greenhouses during forcing.

Premature bud opening can also be related to ethylene. In experiments at Arizona, application of ethephon (an ethylene-releasing chemical) that caused blasting of small (1–2 in.) buds also caused early loss of green color and premature opening of larger (4–5 in.) buds. Under a wide range of growing conditions, 'Nellie White' flowers open when the bud reaches a length of 6.0–6.4 in. (150–160 mm). If buds are significantly smaller than this when opening it would make sense to evaluate your growing area for ethylene contamination. Equipment such as improperly vented heaters or CO_2 burners can easily provide damaging levels of ethylene.

Bud split is an uncommon disorder where the bud is deformed and "splits" along its length (Fig. 24, color plate). Bud split is usually attributed to aphid damage (Post 1941). On the other hand, split buds are often seen with no aphid infestation. Early research (Post 1941) determined that irrigation practice has no influence on bud split, nor does excess fertilizer or temperature fluctuation. Thus, all of the causes of bud split, and their interactions, are not yet known. Aphids, however, do cause the secretion of sugar-rich honeydew that falls to leaves under the aphids. The honeydew provides a growth medium for sooty mold, and greatly reduces the quality of the lily crop.

Leaf epinasty (Fig. 17) can also be caused by ethylene (from ethephon application), by very low greenhouse temperatures, and by reversed greenhouse temperatures (negative DIFs). By returning to a positive or zero DIF, it is possible to regain normal leaf orientation. Since DIF-induced epinasty is reversible, it seems likely that it is a stress response mediated by ethylene.

Bud sunburn. With late Easter dates, the high sunshine level can cause damage to the tender upper leaves and flower buds, especially those in the "puffy" stage. Certainly, this is more of a problem in the Sunbelt than in many other areas. Greenhouse shade reduces or eliminates the problem.

Subdue™ injury (Fig. 25, color plate) was described by Hammer (1985). This injury is uniquely diagnosed by white bleaching of leaf tips, and is easily distinguishable from fluoride leaf scorch (Fig. 20). One Subdue™ application at 4 oz./100 gal. (four times the recommended rate), or two applications at the label rate (1 oz./100 gal.) will cause injury. These are very small volumes, so measurements must be done carefully. Subdue™ is an effective chemical for combating root rot, but label directions must be carefully followed.

Roundup™ injury (Fig. 26, color plates). Roundup™ is often used for weed control in greenhouses. Apparently, lilies are not damaged by direct foliar Roundup™ sprays of 1 lb./acre. Roundup™ injury can occur from root uptake of the herbicide, for example from flood irrigation after Roundup™ application. However, nearly 100× over-application of the Roundup™ was necessary for injury to occur (Weller and Hammer 1984).

Bulb no-shows. Some bulbs never sprout, and are called "no shows." Several explanations may be made. The first is that the bulb may have been slightly sprouted at planting, and the sprout was inadvertently broken during planting. Most bulbs have only one stem and do not recover if the stem is broken. Second, freezing temperatures can kill the shoot while it is still within the bulb. With poor control, bulb freezing can occur in storage. Often, the bulb scales show little damage, but a blistering of the scale epidermis can sometimes be seen. This blistering is associated with small patches of ice under the epidermis. Other evidence of freezing is brown discoloration at the base of the stem seen upon removing scales from the bulb. Third, other environmental factors during storage will affect vernalization rate and thus emergence and growth in the greenhouse. Vernalization requires oxygen, and lack of oxygen or high CO_2 reduces vernalization (Green 1934; Thornton 1939; Chouard 1960). A well-ventilated cooler (vernalization) environment should help alleviate these problems. Ethylene contamination (up to 2 ppm) during bulb vernalization apparently has little effect on crop timing or quality, although bud count may be reduced somewhat (Prince and Cunningham 1991).

Greenhouse Production of Oriental Hybrid Lilies

Introduction

Oriental lilies are complex hybrids of many species, including *L. speciosum, L. japonicum, L. auratum,* and *L. nobilissimum.* Historically, Oriental hybrids were bred for the perennial garden, and many varieties arose from the efforts of scores of amateur hybridizers. As a group, the Orientals may be characterized by large and highly fragrant red, purple, pink, or white flowers on very tall stems that bloom in mid- to late summer.

Interest in growing Orientals as greenhouse forced pot plants has been long standing, but most cultivars are too tall and bloom too late for spring holidays.

General Culture

Most cultural practices are similar to Easter lilies, except as outlined below. Preventative treatment for the root rot complex is critical, and involves regular fungicide applications as described later. Insect and disease problems and their control are the same as for Easter lilies.

Flower Bud Initiation

Flower bud initiation in Oriental hybrid lilies is fundamentally similar to that of Easter lilies. Both groups initiate flowers after vernalization (cold storage), when plants are 4–6 in. tall in the greenhouse. Increasing cold storage hastens emergence and days to flowering in *L. speciosum*, and long days applied at emergence gives the same effect (Weiler 1973). However, a related species (*L. rubellum*) initiates flowers in the fall before cold storage (Niimi and Oda 1989). This diversity of reproductive behavior can be exploited in breeding programs.

Growing Medium, Planting, and Fertilization

There have been no systematic studies on optimum growing media and nutritional characteristics for Oriental hybrids. Most recommendations assume that the requirements are the same as for Easter lilies. A must for all types is a moist but well-drained medium. Thus, peatlite-type mixes of peat, vermiculite, perlite, and styrofoam are commonly used.

Many *Lilium* species that are used in breeding Oriental hybrids (*L. auratum, L. canadense, L. speciosum*) are adapted to acidic, rather that calcareous soils (Bailey 1916; Feldmaier 1970). This suggests that standard, high-pH Easter lily soils may not be best for Oriental hybrids. Additionally, the species *L. auratum, L. japonicum, L. regale,* and *L. speciosum* are classified as stem rooting types (Wister 1930) and usually show very little root development from the bulb base plate when forced in the greenhouse. Plants at the visible bud stage have been observed to have no bulb root development at all. This underscores the importance of using standard depth pots and deep planting to allow as much stem rooting to occur as possible.

Growth Regulators

Oriental hybrids respond to A-Rest™, and drench applications of 0.5–1.0 mg are effective in height control. Bark-based media will tie-up the growth retardant. In Ohio, 1 mg/6-in. pot A-Rest™ drenches reduced 'Sans Souci' height by 17% when applied at emergence or when shoots were 6 in. tall. Sumagic™ is also effective, and at lower rates than A-Rest™. We found that Sumagic™ drenches at 0.05–0.15 mg a.i./pot reduced height of two unnamed Oriental cultivars by 20–40% (Bailey and Miller 1989). Holcomb et al. (1989) found that a combination of pre-plant bulb dips and drench applications (using A-Rest™ or Sumagic™) were more effective than either application alone.

Timing and Forcing Temperatures

Best quality is seen with plants finished at cool temperatures (58°–60°F). Relative to Easter lilies, very little information has been published regarding timing and forcing. It seems to take "forever" for a 'Sans Souci' bud to open, and indeed, bud development on many Oriental hybrid cultivars is much slower than with Easter lilies. Therefore, bud sticks developed for Easter lilies cannot be used on Orientals. Also, within the Oriental hybrid group, there is a large variation in bud development rate after the visible bud stage (Table 19). For this reason, growers should keep accurate cultivar timing records for future reference.

In the Netherlands and other low-light areas, Oriental hybrids respond to supplemental photosynthetic lighting. This treatment, however, is used mainly for cut flowers scheduled for November to February when greenhouse irradiance is lowest. Easter and Mother's Day pot plant forcings would not justify these expensive treatments.

Table 19. Days from visible bud to flowering for three Oriental hybrid lily cultivars at two night temperatures (W. B. Miller and D. A. Bailey, unpublished data).

	Days from visible bud to flowering	
Cultivar	60°F night temp.	65°F night temp.
'A'	55	49
'B'	—	37
'C'	35	32

Post-production Handling

Plants should be marketed when the most mature bud is fully colored, three or four days before opening. Later shipping will cause damage to open flowers in transit, and earlier shipping will increase the incidence of young flower abscission. Plants should be sleeved.

Cultivars

'Sans Souci' and 'Stargazer' are the most common cultivars being forced for pot plant sales. While producing excellent plants, these cultivars are late blooming, and it is impossible to meet the Easter market because of the length of forcing required (usually 140–160 days). Their main use has been for Mother's Day.

New cultivars are being developed both in Europe and in the United States. New Oriental hybrids with major reductions in forcing time have been described (Bailey and Miller 1989). After six weeks of cold storage, these cultivars (Figs. 27a–c, back cover) flowered 85–90 days from planting at 65°F (18.3°C) night temperature. With these and other cultivars, it will be possible to supply the Easter market with a range of unique and colorful Oriental hybrid lilies. Figure 28 (color plate) shows Oriental, Asiatic, and Easter lilies all flowering for the Easter holiday. Certainly, this exciting range of flower color will increase sales potential for all lilies at the Easter holiday.

Major Problems

The biggest problem with Oriental hybrid lilies is abscission and yellowing of lower foliage. The problem is severe with most commercial cultivars, including 'Sans Souci' and 'Stargazer'. The bare lower stem detracts from the intensely colored and attractive flowers. Most Oriental hybrids emerge rapidly soon after planting. This fast emergence, often with no root development, may be a key to solving the lower leaf problem. Without a well-developed root system, the plant will not absorb water and nutrients to drive lower leaf growth. Currently, the solution is to wrap the pot with foil and hide the bare stem. Growing at low temperatures initially will help reduce the rate of stem elongation, and help balance shoot and root growth. A long-term solution will be breeding for new cultivars that show increased basal root development.

Other desired characteristics for potted Oriental hybrid lilies are faster forcing times, upright-facing flowers, and somewhat reduced flower fragrance. Orientals have problems with flower bud abscission, and this could be a major limitation if large-scale production and long shipping is contemplated.

Greenhouse Production of Asiatic Hybrid Lilies

Introduction

This group is familiar for their red, pink, orange, and yellow bright- and pastel-colored flowers. The Mid-Century hybrids that were developed by Jan De Graff at the Oregon Bulb Farm in the years during and after World War II were the staple of pot plant forcing for decades. This group, which includes the well-known cultivars 'Enchantment', 'Joan Evans', 'Harmony', etc., was bred from *L. tigrinum*, *L. dauricum*, *L. wilsonii*, *L. davidii*, and *L. bulbiferum*. Other efforts have led to the yellow Connecticut hybrids ('Connecticut King' and 'Connecticut Lemon Glow') that have been used as pot plant cultivars.

A recent contribution has been the introduction of the Pixie Series from Oregon Bulb Farm. This series contains many colors from red to white, and are genetically dwarf and thus need no growth regulator treatment.

General Culture

For cut flower programs, bulbs are frozen at 28°F (−2.2°C) to reduce additional vernalization and to stop sprouting. Asiatics generally respond well to freezing, although quality loss is inevitable as storage approaches one year. Not all cultivars respond well to freezing, and your bulb broker should be able to recommend specific cultivars for freezing schedules. The bulb grower, shipper, or broker is responsible for the maintenance and monitoring of temperatures in these facilities. With potted plants for the spring market, the bulbs would not have been frozen, but for fall marketing the use of frozen bulbs would be mandatory.

Vernalization and Flower Initiation

The time of flower initiation has been poorly studied for the Asiatic hybrids. It seems likely that initiation occurs much earlier than with Easter lily because some Asiatic hybrids emerge from the soil with flower buds already present. Work with the dwarf Pixie Series indicates that flower initiation can actually occur in the bulb, and that buds are present at the time of planting, as in tulip. Because of the much wider genetic base in the Asiatic group, generalizations are difficult.

Growing Medium, Planting and Fertilization

Three to five bulbs are used in 5–6 in. pots to provide the best foliage and color display. Because many Asiatic hybrid cultivars are susceptible to fluoride-induced leaf scorch, fluoride sources in the media and irrigation water should be avoided, and medium pH adjusted and monitored as described earlier for Easter lilies. Research to determine an optimum fertilization program has not been conducted. Experience indicates a typical Easter lily program is adequate.

Temperatures and Timing

Buds of Asiatic hybrids are much smaller than Easter lilies when they open. For this reason, an Easter lily bud stick cannot be used to time Asiatic cultivars. Most cultivars force in 60 to 95 days at greenhouse night temperatures near 60°F. For most cultivars, it takes about 30 days to flower from the visible bud stage at 60°F night temperature. Optimum plant quality is usually realized a few degrees cooler at about 55°–58° F. Growers should keep accurate temperature and plant development records to establish detailed timing response for cultivars in their own situations.

Height Control

Asiatic hybrids respond to A-Rest™ and probably to Sumagic™. With A-Rest™, drenches and sprays, as well as pre-plant bulb dips are effective. Because of rapidity of early stem growth, drenches at emergence maintain the appearance of lush foliage on the lower stem. Actual rates to use depend on grower location, environmental conditions, and cultivar, but drenches of 0.25–0.75 mg active ingredient usually reduce height 25–50% (Dicks et al. 1974; Simmonds and Cumming 1977). A-Rest™ sprays are usually not effective because of the lack of leaf surface early in forcing. White (1976) found that 100 ppm sprays (spraying 100 ml/pot) reduced Asiatic hybrid height, but cost is prohibitive at these levels. Bulb dips have also been investigated, but, as with Easter lilies, results are variable. For growers interested in experimentation, A-Rest™ dips of 10 ppm for 12 hr. (room temperature) reduced elongation 68% and 82% for 'Enchantment' and 'Harmony', respectively (Simmonds and Cumming 1977). Within the Asiatic hybrid group there are differences in cultivar response, so it is important to keep accurate records for future reference.

Asiatic hybrid lilies have also been shown to stay shorter as a result of mechanical stress (Jerzy and Krause 1980). 'Enchantment' plants shaken for 10 seconds twice a day were 30% shorter than undisturbed plants.

Post-production Handling

Plants should be marketed when the most mature buds are colored, three or four days before opening. Shipping earlier than this increases flower abscission and abortion, and reduces shelf life and consumer appeal. Later shipping will cause damage to open flowers in transit. Plants should be sleeved. Unlike Easter lilies, storage in coolers is limited to a few days due to rapid quality loss.

Cultivars

Many cultivars in a range of colors from white to pink to orange and yellow are available. Consultation with a reputable bulb broker can help decide appropriate cultivars to try. The most commonly grown have been 'Enchantment' (deep orange), 'Connecticut King' (yellow), and 'Red Carpet' (cherry-red). Cultivars of the Pixie Series are rapidly becoming the standard for pot forcing. Some information on these cultivars is given in Table 20. De Hertogh (1989, 1990) has provided information on cut flower and pot plant forcing and should also be consulted.

Major Problems

Asiatic lilies are susceptible to flower bud abscission (bud drop) and flower bud abortion (bud blast). With

Cultural guidelines for cultivars of the 'Pixie' series of dwarf Asiatic hybrid lilies for pot plants.

ltivar	Major color	Finished height (in.)	Weeks to flower by season				Bulb count by bulb size		
			Jan.	Apr.	Jul.	Oct.	10/12	12/14	14/16
ff Pixie	Salmon	15	12	10	8	12	3	6	8
sh Pixie	Orange	18	13	10	8	12	4	6	8
ange Pixie	Orange	15	11	8	6	8	3	4	5
r Pixie	Orange	20	12/13	9	7	9	4	5	7
mmer Pixie	Orange	22	14	1	9	10	4	6	8
n Pixie	Orange	13	12	9	7	11	4	5	7
tter Pixie	Yellow	15	14	11	9	12	3	6	8
lden Pixie	Yellow	18	11	8	6	8	3	3	4
non Pixie	Yellow	15	13/14	0	8	12	3	5	7
imson Pixie	Red	15	12	9	7/8	10	2	3	4
e Pixie	Red	12	12	9	7	11	3	4	5
ugh Pixie	Red	12	10	7	6	8	4	6	8
by Pixie	Red	18	14	1	9	12	4	6	8
ral Pixie	Pink	18	14	2	9	13	3	5	7
wn Pixie	Pink	22	13	0	7	10	3	6	7
ach Pixie	Pink	15	13	1	8	12	5	5	9
k Pixie	Pink	18	12/13	9/10	8	11	3	4	5

ormation supplied by Oregon Bulb Farms. Based on northern Oregon conditions, 55°F NT, 65°F . Plant deep in pots to allow stem roots to form. Suggest using five 10/12s, three 12/14s, or two 16s per 6-in. pot.

'Enchantment', buds are most likely to abscise when they are 0.6–1.6 in. (1.5–4.0 cm) long (Durieux 1975; Durieux et al. 1982). Although flower bud abscission in Asiatic hybrids is closely related to low light levels during winter forcing, the effect is due to increased ethylene formation rather than to reduced carbohydrate production. Plant breeders in the Netherlands have shown that resistance to low-light-induced abscission and abortion has a genetic component, and have made great advances in breeding for low-light tolerant cultivars.

Figure 5. Field of Easter lilies in full flower in mid-July. Note rows on the extreme left have been disbudded to force additional bulb growth.

Figure 6. Field of 'Enchantment' in full flower.

Figure 7. Field and shed operations during lily bulb production: a) digging operations, b) sorting planting stock, c) custom construction of planting equipment, d) planting operations, e) final grading of commercial bulbs, f) finished cases in shed storage.

d

e

f

Figure 12. 'Nellie White' Easter lilies grown experimentally in a recirculating hydroponic system. Top) System showing single 30-gal. solution reservoir, about eight weeks after planting. Middle) Root system and top growth of plants about eight weeks after planting. Bottom) Bench of flowering plants, 15 weeks after planting. A Lesan™ drench was applied two weeks after planting.

Figure 13. Low light levels stretch Easter lilies. Starting about two weeks after emergence, plants were grown for three weeks in (left to right) full sun, 60% shade, or 90% shade.

Figure 17. Mechanical stress can reduce height of Easter lilies. Plants were stressed by running a finger around the leaves 10 times once a day. Treated plants on the right. Note leaf epinasty (downward curling). Treatment began about four weeks before the photo was taken. Flowering was delayed in treated plants by about two weeks.

Figure 19. Whole-plant symptoms of fluoride-induced leaf scorch (fluoride from superphosphate, SP) and reduction of scorch by lime (higher soil pH) in 'Ace'. Left to right: Low SP and low lime; high SP and low lime; low SP and high lime; high SP and high lime. (Photo courtesy of Frank Marousky.)

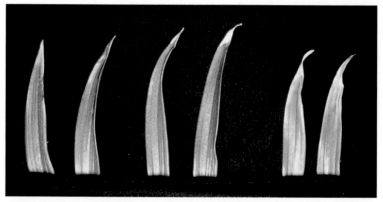

Figure 20. Leaf symptoms of fluoride and boron leaf scorch. The two leaves on the left have fluoride-induced scorch. Note the yellow, chlorotic region near the necrotic (brown). The two middle leaves have boron-induced scorch. Note the lack of chlorotic tissue between the dead area and healthy green leaf tissue. The two right leaves were grown with both fluoride and boron and show the chlorotic area. (Photo courtesy of Frank Marousky).

Figure 21. Lower leaf yellowing and senescence in 'Nellie White'.

Figure 22. Bud abortion. The aborted bud is visible as a small bump at the base of the flower pedicels.

Figure 23. Bud blasting. Two blasted buds on 'Nellie White'. The smallest bud is in the latest stage of "blast." Note shriveling of the bud base in the next largest flower, indicative of early stages of "blast."

Figure 24. Flower split of a mature flower.

Figure 25. Subdue™ injury to 'Nellie White' Easter lilies. Note white bleaching of the leaf tips, a very distinct symptom, as compared to boron or fluoride injury (Fig. 18).

Figure 26. Roundup™ injuries to 'Nellie White' Easter lilies. The chemical was applied to a cement greenhouse floor. It was absorbed by the roots after flood irrigation.

Figure 28. Flowering lily varieties at Easter.

Insect Pests and Diseases of Lilies

Insects

Below are brief descriptions of the common insects found on forced lilies, with suggestions for control following the descriptions.

APHIDS

Aphids are commonly seen during lily production. Several types, including the melon aphid (*Aphis gossypii*), green peach aphid (*Myzus persicae*), foxglove aphid (*Acyrthosiphon solani*), crescent-marked aphid (*Neomyzus circumflexus*), bean aphid (*Aphis fabae*), potato aphid (*Macrosiphum euphorbiae*), purple-spotted aphid (*Macrosiphum lilii*), crescent-marked lily aphid (*Neomyzus circumflexus*), and pale-yellow aphid (*Macrosiphum scoliopi*) have all been reported on lilies (Pennell and Johnson 1967; Baker 1990). Aphids may cause direct damage, including splitting of developing buds and stunting and curling of young foliage, especially with the foxglove aphid. The honeydew secreted by aphids is rich in carbohydrate and amino acids, providing a nutrient source for sooty molds. In addition, most aphids (especially the melon aphid) are vectors for one or more virus diseases, and may spread disease from infected to healthy plants.

BULB MITES

Bulb mites (*Rhizoglyphus robini*) are present on most or all bulbs. They are easy to see and have short, stubby legs, with white bodies about 1/32-in. long. The mites feed on the dead and decaying tissues of outer, older scales. Plants that have been weakened by virus infection or *Fusarium* decay may be attacked directly, but healthy bulbs are not generally attacked by the bulb mite and are not a major concern of lily forcers (Pennell and Johnson 1967). It has been noted that high populations of bulb mites (more than 300 per bulb) increase the severity of root rot, and reduce the effectiveness of preventative fungicidal drenches (Ascerno 1989). These high populations, however, would not be expected each year. The usual control measure is a pre-plant bulb soak using kelthane. Other materials, such as Avid™ and Vendex™, drenched after potting at label rates, may hold promise as alternatives to kelthane, but more research is necessary (Ascerno 1989). A non-chemical control method is to soak bulbs for 30 min. in 110°F water (Pennell and Johnson 1967). Accurate temperature control is essential to minimize extensive bulb damage (Baker 1990). Many growers do not treat for this pest and have not experienced trouble.

OTHER INSECTS

Other insect pests have been reported on lilies: lily beetle (*Liliceris lilii*), rove beetle (*Apocellus sphaericollis*), spotted cucumber beetle (*Diabrotica undecimpunctata howardia*), lily weevil (*Agasphaerops nigra*), narcissus bulb fly (*Merodon equestris*), lesser bulb fly (*Eumerus tuberculatus*), red banded leaf roller (*Argyrotaenia velutinana*), garden centipede (*Scutigerella immaculata*), eastern lubber grasshopper (*Romalea microptera*), grape mealybug (*Pseudococcus maritimus*), spotted millipede (*Blanjulus guttulatus*), roach (*Pycnoscelus surinamensis*), Florida red scale (*Chrysomphalus aonidum*), stalk borer (*Papaipema nebris*), stem borers (*Neolasioptera hibisci* and *Emboloecia sauzalita*), banded greenhouse thrips (*Hercinothrips femoralis*), flower thrips (*Franklinella tritici*), lily bulb thrips (*Liothrips vaneekei*), slugs, and grubs of the May and June beetles (Pennell and Johnson 1967). Fungus gnats are another problem, especially when plants are grown in highly organic media. With the exception of aphids, most of the above insects are not major economic pests on greenhouse-forced lilies.

NON-CHEMICAL CONTROL

It should be pointed out that, with the exception of bulb mites, lily bulbs start out insect-free. Certainly aphids are not present on the bulbs. Thus, pests that develop during forcing are the result of migration from nearby crops or weeds. Eggs carried in soil and plant residue, adults hitch-hiking on workers' clothing, or adults being aspirated into the greenhouse by fans are probably the most common ways lilies become infested with aphids. Fastidious attention to sanitation and screening vents are both very useful practices. Aphids are attracted to yellow sticky cards, and these should be hung in the crop and monitored regularly. Also, workers should avoid yellow clothing to minimize transmission between greenhouses.

CHEMICAL INSECT CONTROL

The guidelines given in Table 21 are for informational purposes only, and are not intended to be recommendations. The user bears the responsibility to check and understand product labels, and to apply all agricultural chemicals according to the manufacturer's guidelines. It is illegal to use any agricultural chemical in a manner inconsistent with its labeling. Check with your local extension specialist because some chemicals may not be approved in certain states or counties.

Table 21. Insecticides effective against aphids, bulb mites, and fungus gnats, the major arthropod pests of Easter lily.

Common name	Brand name	Rate	Application method
Aphids			
Acephate	Orthene™ 75SP	5–10 oz./100 gal.	High volume spray
Bifenthrin	Talstar™ 10WP	6–24 oz./100 gal.	High volume spray
Cyfluthrin	Tempo™ 2EC	1–2 oz./100 gal.	High volume spray
Diazinon	Knox-Out™ 2FM (micro-encapsulated)	3–6 pt./100 gal.	High volume spray
Dichlorvos	Vapona™ 4EC	See label	Smoke or fog[1]
d-Phenothrin	Sumithrin™ 2EC	1–2 pt./100 gal.	High volume spray
Endosulfan	Thiodan™ 50WP	16 oz./100 gal.	High volume spray
	Thiodan™ 3EC	0.67 qt./100 gal.	High volume spray
Fluvalinate	Mavrik™ 2F	2–5 oz./100 gal.	High volume spray
Malathion	Fogging formulation	See label	Fog
	Malathion™ 25WP	2 lb./100 gal.	High volume spray
	Malathion™ 55EC	1 pt./100 gal.	High volume spray
Naled	Dibrom™ 60 EC	See label	Apply as a fumigant to steam pipes
Oxamyl	Oxamyl™ 10G	0.25–0.5 tsp./pot	Apply granules to soil surface
	Vydate™ 24L	1–4 pt./100 gal.	High volume spray or drench
Resmethrin	SBP-1382	1 pt./100 gal.	High volume spray
Soap	Safer™ Soap	8–20 pt./100 gal.	High volume spray
Sulfotepp	Dithio™ or dithione	1 lb./50,000 cu. ft.	Smoke
Bulb mites			
Chlorpyrifos	Dursban™ 50WP	8–16 oz./100 gal.	30 minute preplant bulb soak
Dicofol	Kelthane™ 35WP	2 oz./10 gal.	30 minute pre-plant bulb soak
Dienochlor	Pentac™ 50WP	8 oz./100 gal.	High volume spray
	Pentac Aquaflow™	0.5 pt./100 gal.	High volume spray
Fluvalinate	Mavrik™ 2F	See label	Bulb dip
Oxamyl	Oxamyl™ 10G	0.25–0.5 tsp./pot	Apply granules to soil surface
	Vydate™ 24L	1–4 pt./100 gal.	High volume spray or drench
Fungus gnats (adults)			
Dichlorvos	Vapona™ 4EC	See label	Smoke or fog[1]
Resmethrin	SBP-1382	See label	Aerosol, fog, or spray[2]
Sulfotepp	Dithio™ or dithione	1 lb./50,000 cu. ft.	Smoke

Common name	Brand name	Rate	Application method
Diazinon	Pt 265 Knox-Out™	See label	Fog
	Pt 265 Knox-Out™	3–6 pt./100 gal.	High volume spray
Malathion	Malathion 57EC, or 50	1 tsp./gal.	Growing medium surface spray (150 sq. ft.)
Naled	Dibrom™ 60EC	See label	Apply as a fumigant on steam pipes
Kinoprene	Enstar™ 5E	6 fl oz./100 gal.	High volume spray at bi-weekly intervals
Fungus gnats (larvae)			
Diazinon	Diazinon™ 50WP	2 lb./100 gal.	Soil drench
Bacillus thuringiensis	Gnatrol™	1–8 pt./100 gal.	Soil drench
Oxamyl	Oxamyl™ 10G	0.25–0.5 tsp./pot	Apply granules to soil surface
	Vydate™ 2SL	1–4 pt./100 gal.	Soil drench

[1] Most effective at 60°–65°F.
[2] Most effective at 50°–72°F. Rapid control but with short residual life.

These general guidelines have been adapted from several published sources and are provided for informational purposes only, and are not intended to be recommendations. The user bears the responsibility to check and understand product labels, and to apply all agricultural chemicals according to manufacturer's guidelines. It is illegal to use any agricultural chemical in a manner inconsistent with its labeling. Check with your local extension specialist because some chemicals may not be approved in certain states or counties.

Diseases

FUNGUS DISEASES

Root rot complex (primarily *Pythium, Rhizoctonia,* and *Fusarium*) is the most important problem in greenhouse forcing of all lilies. Basal and stem roots can be damaged by root rots. Basal root rot is usually responsible for rapid yellowing of lower foliage in the later stages of forcing. Plants grown in poorly-drained mixes are more likely to succumb to root rot, as are plants watered too frequently. Easter lilies and some hybrid lilies have stem roots which begin developing about the time of flower bud initiation. These stem roots are often responsible for the maintenance of a good quality crop after the basal system has been weakened or destroyed.

The best prevention against root rot is a porous, well-drained potting medium, proper watering, and a regular schedule of fungicidal drenches. Since the root rot complex involves several organisms, a range of fungicides must be used regularly for control. *Pythium* is suppressed by Subdue™, Truban™ and Terrazole™. *Rhizoctonia* and *Fusarium* are suppressed by Benlate™, Tersan™, or Cleary's 3336-F™. A successful drench program for root rot control is given in Table 22.

Table 22. Fungicidal drench schedule for root rot control in lilies.

At planting, drench with one group 1 fungicide (below) *and* with quintozene (Terraclor™) at 4 oz./100 gal.

At monthly intervals, drench with a combination of one fungicide from each of the groups below:

Group 1. *Pythium* control.
Etridiazole	Truban™ 30 WP at 3–10 oz./100 gal. drench.
	Truban™ 25 EC at 4–8 oz./100 gal. drench.
	Terrazole™ 4 EC at 2–4 oz./100 gal. drench.
	Terrazole™ 35 WP at 3–10 oz./100 gal. drench.
Metalaxyl[1]	Subdue™ 2 E at 1 oz./100 gal. drench.
Propamocarb	Banol™ 65% EC, 20 oz./100 gal. drench.

Group 2. *Rhizoctonia* and *Fusarium* control.
Benomyl	Benlate™ 50 DF at 1 lb./100 gal. drench.
Thiophanate-methyl	Cleary's 3336-4F™ at 1.5 pt./100 gal. drench.

[1]Subdue can cause leaf tip burning (Fig. 23) when used above the recommended rate, or with multiple applications of the recommended rate. Many growers have had good control and no injury with 2 drenches of 0.5 oz./100 gal.

These general guidelines have been adapted from several published sources and are provided for informational purposes only, and are not intended to be recommendations. The user bears the responsibility to check and understand product labels, and to apply all agricultural chemicals according to manufacturer's guidelines. It is illegal to use any agricultural chemical in a manner inconsistent with its labeling. Check with your local extension specialist because some chemicals may not be approved in certain states or counties.

Grey mold (*Botrytis cinerea*) can be a major problem with forced plants. The disease is encouraged by cool, wet conditions in the greenhouse. Spores are present on dead plant tissues, and are carried by splashing water or by any means of physical movement of infected, spore-covered debris. The mycelium grows best at low temperatures (40°–45°F). Thus, *Botrytis* usually is not a problem during greenhouse forcing, but growers should be careful when holding advanced plants in very cool greenhouses or in a cooler prior to sale. In addition, holding plants under low light levels (e.g., in a cooler) increases their susceptibility to *Botrytis* (Agrios 1978). During cold storage of budded plants, *Botrytis* is prevented by appropriate fungicidal treatments (see Table 23). Use extreme care to avoid getting water on the foliage or flower buds if irrigation is necessary in the cooler. If possible, reducing the relative humidity of the cooler is helpful. Essentially, creating constant air movement and making sure the foliage is dry into the night avoids most problems with *Botrytis*.

Table 23. Fungicides effective against *Botrytis* on flower buds and leaves during storage.

Chlorothalonil	Daconil™ 2787 4F, 2 pt./100 gal. high volume spray. Daconil™ 75 WP, 1 lb. WP/100 gal. spray. Exotherm Termil™ 20 Fumigation smoke (leaves no residue on flowers and leaves).
Benomyl	Benlate™ 50DF, 8 oz./100 gal.
Iprodione	Chipco 26019™ 50 WP, 1 lb./100 gal.
Vinclozolin	Ornalin™ 50 WP, 8 oz./100 gal.
Thiophanate-Methyl	Cleary's 3336-4F™, 1.5 pt./100 gal.
Mancozeb	Manzate™ 75DF, 1–2 lb./100 gal.

These general guidelines have been adapted from several published sources and are provided for informational purposes only, and are not intended to be recommendations. The user bears the responsibility to check and understand product labels, and to apply all agricultural chemicals according to manufacturer's guidelines. It is illegal to use any agricultural chemical in a manner inconsistent with its labeling. Check with your local extension specialist because some chemicals may not be approved in certain states or counties.

Lily botrytis (*Botrytis elliptica*) is a serious disease in field-grown plants, but is rarely a problem in the greenhouse. This foliar disease causes tip, marginal, and entire leaf necrosis, especially after anthesis in the field. In years past, it was not uncommon to see entire fields wiped out by this "fire" disease. It is likely that both *Botrytis* species are involved in the total field disease syndrome (McWhorter 1957). If blooms are not removed, they will droop on the upper leaves, allowing moisture to be retained and initiating disease. Senescent flowers are often a point of entry for the disease. The primary control is by application of copper-containing Bordeaux fungicides.

VIRUS DISEASES

Cucumber mosaic and lily symptomless virus may be present in Easter lilies. These viruses are transmitted by aphids in production fields on the West Coast. High concentration of the cucumber mosaic virus causes leaf fleck (splotchy yellow areas on leaves). Plants free of the symptomless virus have been developed through tissue culture methods at Oregon State University by Dr. Thomas C. Allen. Plants free of this virus are taller and generally more vigorous, but flower number is not consistently increased.

OTHER DISEASES

Anthracnose or "black scale" (*Collectotrichum lilii*) was serious in the Louisiana bulb industry with the 'Creole' lily prior to the 1950s (McWhorter 1957). A milder form called "brown scale" is present on Northwest native lilies and has been seen in West Coast fields, but it has not developed into a production problem. Dimmock and Tammen (1967) reported an anthracnose flower disease, but this has not been a recurring problem in recent years.

Stem or "mud" rot (*Phytopthora parsitica* and *P. cactorium*) is a historical problem that occurred when soil was washed (naturally or from cultivation) into the crowns of young plants. This disease has been essentially eliminated from West Coast production fields by the practice of planting in raised rows.

Basal rot (*Fusarium*), once a threat to the developing West Coast bulb industry, is now only occasionally found. The rot develops after prolonged bulb storage, especially under warm conditions. Occasionally *Fusarium* is seen during scale propagation in warm conditions (McWhorter 1957). *Fusarium* is a problem on Oriental hybrid lilies.

Scale tip rot is often associated with *Rhizopus* (bread mold fungus), and was a greater problem with the 'Croft' cultivar than with modern cultivars. Incidence of scale tip rot was not associated with any nutritional deficiencies, including micronutrients (McWhorter 1957).

Scale pitting seen on outer lily scales is often a combination of an initial *Rhizoctonia* infection followed by damage by bulb mites. The yellow pigmentation seen on other scales is also attributed to minor infections of *Rhizoctonia*.

Rust (*Uromycetes holwayi*) is found on lilies, and was a common problem in the 1930s. Sanitation and rouging were instrumental in eliminating the problem.

Sclerotinium bulb rot (*Sclerotium*) can be severe on *Lilium regale*, but rarely is seen on *L. longiflorum* or *L. speciosum* (McWhorter 1957).

Blue mold (*Penicillium corymbiferum*) is a storage rot seen on Oriental hybrid lilies. Early experiments with *Lilium speciosum* showed that shoot growth was reduced in greater proportion to level of infection, indicating that this is a severely debilitating problem (McWhorter 1957).

DISEASE CONTROL

When pesticide or growth regulator guidelines are given, the reader must be aware that they are presented for informational purposes only. No endorsement is intended for products mentioned, nor is criticism meant for products not mentioned. Before purchasing and using any agricultural chemical, all labels must be checked for registered use, rates, and application frequency. It is illegal to use any pesticide in a manner inconsistent with its labeling.

Costs of Producing Easter and Hybrid Lilies

As in any other greenhouse crop, profitable Easter lily production lies in understanding and managing both direct (materials and assignable labor) and indirect (overhead) components of the crop. Lilies can be a highly labor-intensive crop, depending upon the final plant quality desired. Much of the labor costs are associated with spacing and moving plants to control height and development rate. On the other hand, many growers do very little sorting or moving, yet produce crops that are readily saleable in their particular markets. Obviously, these firms will have lower labor costs than ones that sort and move their lilies extensively.

In the following examples, assumptions have been made regarding costs of and inputs to production. These numbers should not be used directly in your operation; rather, the format is a guide for developing relevant, specific costs for your own use. Let us assume that we are producing a crop of 10,000 6-in. lilies, starting with 8–9 in. bulbs ($0.95 each), with a spacing of 2.5 pots/sq. ft. in a 20,000 sq. ft. greenhouse with 15,000 sq. ft. of bench area (75% benching efficiency), and a 17-week (119-day) crop time.

The first task is to estimate the overhead costs per square foot of growing area per week (sq. ft./week cost). This cost includes all overhead items that are not directly assignable to any specific crop throughout the year. From Table 24, we arrive at a cost of $0.1576 per square foot for each week the crop is in the greenhouse. This number is the basis for determining total overhead costs assignable to the crop.

After the overhead cost is determined, the total production costs of overhead and direct cost can be calculated for the crop (Table 25). The costs for items such as pots, sleeves, shipping boxes, A-Rest™, etc. can be gleaned from invoices. Labor costs are best determined from time sheets. In the example below, data from a cost study by

Table 24. Determining cost/sq. ft./week for growing Easter lilies.

Assumptions: A crop of 10,000 lilies, 8–9 in. bulbs, 2.5 pots/sq. ft., 20,000 sq. ft. gree house (75% benching efficiency), 17-week crop time.

Line	Item	Cost from greenhouse records ($)	Less sum of costs directly related to lilies ($)	Overhead cost ($)
1.	Salaries and wages			50,000
2.	Bulbs @ $0.95	9500	9500	
3.	Pots @ $0.15 ea.	1500	1500	
4.	Media @ $0.12/pot	1200	1200	
5.	Fertilizer, pesticides, and PGR's @ $0.23/pot	2300	2300	
6.	Repairs and maintenance			4000
7.	Other direct costs (foil, sleeves, etc). @ $0.355/pot	3550	3550	
8.	Total direct costs to lilies		18,050	
9.	Utilities (heat, phone, sewer, etc.)			30,000
10.	Administrative and selling costs			4000
11.	Fixed overhead (insurance, rent taxes, depreciation)			15,000
12.	Total unallocated			103,000
13.	Investment in greenhouse		100,000	
14.	Desired rate of return		0.20	
15.	Unallocated return on investment (13 × 14)			20,000
16.	Total unallocated costs (15 + 12)			123,000
17.	Net growing area (sq. ft.)			15,000
18.	Unallocated costs/sq. ft./yr. Line 16 / Line 17)			8.2
19.	Weeks in operation			52
20.	Unallocated cost/sq. ft./week Line 18 / Line 19)			0.157

Brumfield et al. (1981) were used for labor costs. In that study, labor was calculated through time and motion studies, with a range of 105 to 204 seconds per pot for all labor items. In this example, we will use the worst-case scenario of 200 seconds per pot.

Our lily cost $2.88 per pot to grow, sleeve, and box for shipping. Transportation costs are not included in this estimate. Also, an optimistic 0% loss was assumed. When a 10% loss (a reasonable loss due to late or early plants, non-sprouting bulbs, etc.) is included, the cost/pot increases to $3.20. For 10,000 pots, the total crop cost is $32,000. It is disturbing to see how loss percentage affects the final cost of each plant (Table 26).

Since the goal is to make a profit, a selling price must still be established. Ideally, selling price is determined by choosing a desired profit and then calculating the required selling price to realize appropriate profit.

Table 25. Determining total production costs for an Easter lily.

Direct costs

Row 1.	Sum of direct costs	$18,050	Sum of DC (line 8)
Row 2.	Number of units	10,000	
Row 3.	Direct cost/pot	$1.805	Row 1 / Row 2

Overhead costs

Row 4.	Space/unit (sq. ft.)	0.400	Based on 2.5 pots/sq. ft.
Row 5.	Space/crop (sq. ft.)	4000	Row 2 × Row 4
Row 6.	Time (weeks)	17	Crop time on bench
Row 7.	Space × weeks	68,000	Row 5 × Row 6
Row 8.	Cost/sq. ft./week	$0.157	Overhead/ft./wk., line 20
Row 9.	Total crop overhead	$10,717	Row 8 × row 7
Row 10.	Overhead, per pot	$1.072	Row 9 / Row 2
Row 11.	Total cost/unit	$2.877	Direct + OH, Rows 3 + 10
Row 12.	Percent saleable	0.90	Accounts for loss, etc.
Row 13.	Adjusted cost/pot	$3.20	Row 11 / Row 12

Direct cost assumptions per plant (as of 1990):
Pot $0.150   Quantity price (includes $0.01 shipping cost).
Soil mix $0.120   Pro Mix™, 5.5 cu ft bale @ $19.25 per bale, (filling 160 pots per bale).
Sleeve $0.085   (includes $0.005 for shipping).
Fertilizer $0.02.

Table 26. Effect of percentage of non-saleable plants on final plant cost, assuming an initial cost of $2.88/plant.

	Percent Unsaleable									
	0%	5%	7%	10%	13%	15%	20%	25%	30%	40%
Final cost, $/plant	2.88	3.03	3.10	3.20	3.31	3.39	3.60	3.84	4.11	4.80

Many people fail to realize that profit is calculated from the selling price, not the cost. Therefore, selling price is determined by the following formula:

$$\frac{\text{Cost per pot}}{(1 - \text{profit})}$$

So, if a 20% profit is desired on a per plant cost of $3.20, the selling price must be $3.20/(1−.20) = $4.00 per pot. Table 27 gives factors used to determine selling price.

Table 27. Profit factors for achieving desired profits on sales.

	Profit percentage desired								
	4%	7%	10%	12%	15%	20%	25%	30%	35%
Multiply final cost by ⟶ to obtain selling price.	1.042	1.075	1.111	1.136	1.176	1.25	1.333	1.429	1.538

104

The Future

The Industry

In general, the United States floriculture industry is in for a lot of changes. New and better ways of crop production are being developed, and will continue to be developed. The application of "old-fashioned" techniques of crop growth control (nutrient, light, and temperature stress) will be increasingly refined and will allow significant reductions in crop inputs. These research areas will have a major impact on the environmental stewardship of the entire industry, not just with lily production.

I predict that in five years we will have only 50% of the chemicals currently available for use in greenhouses on ornamental plants. Floriculture is a "minor use" industry, and the chemical companies cannot afford to maintain labels on many materials useful to this industry. This being the case, innovations in crop protection must occur on a regular basis. I foresee greater use of rational biological control systems that will be more forgiving to the grower: systems where a carefully developed predator population will not be wiped out by an incorrect application of some chemical; systems that will allow reduced pesticide applications, yielding better plant quality at lower cost.

We will continue to see more greenhouses with the capability for recirculating irrigation water, leading to reduced water use and greenhouse runoff. New controlled fertilizer products will appear to aid in fertilizer leaching into groundwater. Lilies will be grown using all of these innovations, and our creativity and crop management skills will increase.

Lilies

An announcement that caught the attention of many in the floriculture world was the new Oglevee Associates process for producing flowering Easter lilies without bulb forcing (Tammen et al. 1986). Basically, bulblets are regenerated from leaf cuttings from virus-free plants and planted. After five to seven months, three weeks of long days are given to cause bolting and floral induction. Flowering occurs about 75 days after the start of long days.

Although the process has been tested on a pilot commercial scale, it has not proven to produce consistent commercially acceptable crops. Much more work needs to be done before commercial acceptance is gained since the final plants are not of the highest "florist quality" that most retail customers desire.

This same approach is feasible from seed, stem bulblets, and aerial bulbils. Vegetative propagules or seedlings are grown under non-inductive short days (8 hr.) until they are large enough to support stem-bolting and flower formation. This usually takes six to eight months. Three weeks of long days (16 hr.) are given to begin, but not fully complete, flower initiation. Plants are returned to short days for three weeks, then a final three-week long-day period completes flower initiation (Ascher 1974).

The single most important area of lily research in the next 20 years should be breeding and crop improvement. A review of the Dutch effort in lily breeding reveals staggering progress in the development of cultivars that are especially suited to production conditions in the Netherlands. These efforts have included "Easter lily" types as well as hybrid types. For example, hybrid cultivars have been developed for the ability to grow in low light without aborting flower buds, and for disease resistance.

Post-production quality is another important issue in the lily industry. Lower leaf senescence and flower quality and longevity are specific areas that need more research. In particular, the common practice of storing "budded" Easter lily plants in coolers prior to sale is very detrimental to plant quality. We must learn the reasons for this, then develop techniques to stop the problem.

The common cultivars of Asiatic and Oriental hybrids continue to suffer from seasonal flower bud abscission. In addition to the breeding effort noted above, we need to find out more about the physiological processes involved in hybrid flower bud abscission.

In summary, the future research needs of the floricultural industry are many. This is no small task, as the cost of research and development is astronomical. The industry must become a staunch supporter of applied and basic floricultural research. Research built the foundations of the industry, and it is now time for the industry to shore up the foundations of the crumbling research structure. The "new generation" of floricultural researchers are as good as, if not better than, ever before. The problems we face, however, are staggering compared to any other time. Through industry and university cooperation, where good ideas are exchanged and acted upon, progress will be made to the benefit of all.

Appendix:
Useful Conversions

°F	°C	in.	cm	ft.	meters
30	−1.1	1	2.5	1	0.3
35	1.7	2	5.1	2	0.6
40	4.4	3	7.6	3	0.9
45	7.2	4	10.2	4	1.2
50	10.0	5	12.7	5	1.5
55	12.8	6	15.2	6	1.8
60	15.6	7	17.8	7	2.1
65	18.3	8	20.3	8	2.4
70	21.1	9	22.9	9	2.7
75	23.9	10	25.4	10	3.0
80	26.7	11	27.9		
85	29.4	12	30.5		
90	32.2				

Foot-candles	Lux	PPF ($\mu mol \cdot m^2 \cdot sec^1$)
1000	10,800	200
2000	21,500	400
3000	32,400	600
4000	43,100	800
5000	53,900	1000
6000	64,700	1200
7000	75,500	1400
8000	86,300	1600
9000	97,100	1800
10,000	107,900	2000

Gal.	liters	oz.	grams	lbs.	grams
0.25	0.95	1	28.4	0.5	226.8
0.50	1.89	2	65.7	1.0	453.6
0.75	2.84	3	85.1	1.5	680.4
1.0	3.79	4	113.4	2.0	907.2
2.0	7.57	8	226.8	2.5	1134.0
		12	340.2		
		16	453.6		

fl. oz.	ml	oz./100 gal.	mg/l	lbs./100 gal.	g/l
1	29.6	1	74.9	0.5	0.6
2	59.2	2	149.8	1.0	1.2
3	88.7	3	224.7	1.5	1.8
4	118.3	4	229.6	2.0	2.4
8	236.6	8	599.1	2.5	3.0
12	354.9	12	898.7		
16	473.2	16	1198.3		

References

Agricultural Statistics Board. 1991. *United States Dept. Agric. Floriculture Crops. 1990 Summary.* Special Circ. 6–1 (1991). 78 pp.

Agrios, G. N. 1978. *Plant Pathology.* Academic Press. New York, N.Y.

Anonymous. 1973. *Ohio Flor. Assn. Bul.* 528:2.

Anonymous. 1988. Water quality: Effects on nutritional management. *Techn. Bull. PTB-133,* Grace Horticultural Products, Fogelsville, Penn. 18051.

Ascerno, M. E. 1989. Untitled. *GrowerTalks* 53(6):134.

Ascher, P. D. 1974. Thoughts on rapid flowering and increased bud count from trumpet lily seedlings. *Yrbk. North Amer. Lily Soc.* 27:96–97.

Baker, J. R. 1990. An update on Easter lily insect and mite control. *North Carolina Flr. Growers Bull.* 35(1):11–13.

Bailey, D. A., and W. B. Miller. 1989. Response of Oriental hybrid lilies to ancymidol and uniconazole. *HortScience* 24:519.

Bailey, L. H. 1916. Lilium. pp. 1862–1864. In: *The Standard Cyclopedia of Horticulture.* Vol. 4. Macmillian.

Blaney, L. T., D. E. Hartley, and A. N. Roberts. 1965. Flower count compared to total bulb weight. *Oregon Orn. and Nurs. Digest.* 9(2):1–2.

Brumfield, R. G., P. V. Nelson, A. J. Coutu, D. H. Willitts, and R. S. Sowell. 1981. Cost of producing Easter lilies in North Carolina. *J. Amer. Soc. Hort. Sci.* 106:561–564.

Catholic Almanac. 1989. Our Sunday Visitor, Inc. Huntington, IN. p. 246.

Chouard, P. 1960. Vernalization and its relations to dormancy. *Ann. Rev. Plant Physiol.* 11:191–237.

De Hertogh, A. A. 1989. *Holland Bulb Forcer's Guide, 4th ed.* Intl. Flower-Bulb Centre. Hillegrom, The Netherlands.

De Hertogh, A. A. 1990. Research on forced flower bulbs focuses on improved quality and cultivars. *PPGA News.* 21(11):2–7.

De Hertogh, A. A., and N. Blakely. 1972. Influence of gibberellins A_3 and A_{4+7} on development of forced *Lilium longiflorum* Thunb. cv. Ace. *J. Amer. Soc. Hort. Sci.* 97:320–323.

De Hertogh, A. A., W. H. Carlson, and S. Kays. 1969. Controlled temperature forcing of planted lily bulbs. *J. Amer. Soc. Hort. Sci.* 94:433–436.

De Hertogh, A. A., H. P. Rasmussen, and N. Blakely. 1976. Morphological changes and factors influencing shoot apex development of *Lilium longiflorum* Thunb. during forcing. *J. Amer. Soc. Hort. Sci.* 101:463–471.

Dicks, J. W., J. M. Gilford, and A. R. Rees. 1974. The influence of timing of application and gibberellic acid on the effects of ancymidol on growth and flowering of mid-century hybrid lily cv. Enchantment. *Scientia Hortic.* 2:153–163.

Dimmock, A. W., and J. Tammen. 1967. Diseases. In: D. C. Kiplinger and R. W. Langhans (eds.), *Lilies. The Culture, Diseases, Insects and Economics of Easter Lilies.* Cornell Univ. Press, Ithaca, N.Y.

Durieux, A. J. B. 1975. Additional lighting of lilies (cv. Enchantment) in the winter to prevent flower-bud abscission. *Acta Hortic.* 47:237–240.

Durieux, A. J. B., G. A. Kamerbeek, and U. Van Meeteren. 1982. The existence of a critical period for the abscission and a non-critical period for blasting of flower buds of *Lilium* 'Enchantment'; Influence of light and ethylene. *Scientia Hortic.* 18:287–297.

Einert, A. E., and C. O. Box. 1967. Effects of light intensity on flower bud abortion and plant growth of *Lilium longiflorum. Proc. Amer. Soc. Hort. Sci.* 90:427–432.

Erwin, J., R. Heins, R. Berghage, M. Karlsson, W. Carlson, and J. Biernbaum. 1988. Why grow plants with warmer nights than days? *GrowerTalks* 51(12):48–58.

Erwin, J. E., R. D. Heins, M. Karlsson, R. Berghage, W. Carlson, and J. Biernbaum. 1987. The basics on Easter lilies: Light and temperature. *GrowerTalks* 51(7):84–90.

Erwin, J. E., R. D. Heins, and M. G. Karlsson. 1989. Thermomorphogenesis in *Lilium longiflorum. Amer. J. Bot.* 76:47–52.

Feldmaier, C. 1970. *Lilies.* Arco Publ. Co., New York, N.Y.

Gianfagna, T. J., and G. J. Wulster. 1986. Comparative effects of ancymidol and paclobutrazole on Easter lily. *HortScience* 21:463–464.

Green, D. E. 1934. Decay of lily bulbs during storage. *Lily Yrbk.* pp. 79–81.

Green, J. L. 1986. Bulb production in the Northwest. *Ornamentals Northwest Newsletter* 10(2):2, 22.

Griffiths, D. 1930. The production of lily bulbs. *U.S. Dept. Agric. Circ.* 102.

Hammer, P. A. 1985. Growing ideas. *GrowerTalks* 49(2):16.

Heins, R., J. Erwin, M. Karlsson, R. Berghage, W. Carlson, and J. Biernbaum. 1987. Tracking Easter lily height with graphs. *GrowerTalks* 51(8):64–68.

Heins, R. D., H. B. Pemberton, and H. F. Wilkins. 1982a. The influence of light on lily (*Lilium longiflorum* Thunb.). I. Influence of light intensity on plant development. *J. Amer. Soc. Hort. Sci.* 107:330–335.

Heins, R. D., H. F. Wilkins and W. E. Healy. 1982b. The influence of light on lily (*Lilium longiflorum* Thunb.). II. Influence of photoperiod and light stress on flower number, height, and growth rate. *J. Amer. Soc. Hort. Sci.* 107:335–338.

Hiraki, Y., and Y. Ota. 1975. The relationship between growth inhibition and ethylene production by mechanical stimulation in *Lilium longiflorum*. *Plant Cell Physiol.* 16:185–189.

Holcomb, E. J., J. W. White, and D. J. Beattie. 1989. Adaption of 'Sans Souci' lilies to potted plant culture. *Acta Hortic.* 252:159–171.

Jerzy, M., and J. Krause. 1980. Two factors controlling growth and flowering of forced lilies 'Enchantment': Light intensity and mechanical stress. *Acta Hortic.* 109:111–115.

Jiao, J., M. J. Tsujita, and D. P. Murr. 1986. Effects of paclobutrazol and A-rest on growth, flowering, leaf carbohydrate, and leaf senescence in 'Nellie White' Easter lily (*Lilium longiflorum* Thunb). *Scientia Hortic.* 30:135–141.

Karlsson, M. G., R. D. Heins, and J. E. Erwin. 1988. Quantifying temperature-controlled leaf unfolding rates in 'Nellie White' Easter lily. *J. Amer. Soc. Hort. Sci.* 113:70–74.

Kiplinger, D. C. 1953. Temperature and light intensity during forcing on 'Croft' lilies. *Ohio Flor. Assoc. Bul.* 291:2.

Kohl, H. C. 1967. Correlation between rate of leaf initiation and apex diameter of *Lilium longiflorum* cultivar 'Ace'. *HortScience* 2:15–16.

Kohl, H. C., and R. L. Nelson. 1963. Daylength and light intensify as independent factors in determining height in Easter lilies. *Proc. Amer. Soc. Hort. Sci.* 83:808–810.

Lange, N., and R. Heins. 1990. The lowdown on how bulb size influences lily development. *GrowerTalks* 53:52–53.

Langhans, R. W., J. C. Neal, J. G. Seeley, T. C. Weiler, J. P. Sanderson, R. K. Horst, and M. Daughtery. 1990.

114

Cornell Greenhouse Crop Production Guideline for New York State. Integrated Crop Management for Lilies. 24 pp.

Langhans, R. W., and D. R. Smith. 1966. Lily bulb size. *New York Flr. Grow. Bull.* 242:8.

Langhans, R. W., and T. C. Weiler. 1967. Factors affecting flowering. In: D. C. Kiplinger and R. W. Langhans (eds.), *Lilies. The Culture, Diseases, Insects and Economics of Easter Lilies.* Cornell Univ. Press, Ithaca, N.Y.

Larson, R. A., and C. Beth Thorne. 1988. Bulb dips may not control lily height. *Greenhouse Grower* 6(1):92–96.

Lewis, A. J., and J. S. Lewis. 1982. Height control of *Lilium longiflorum* Thunb. 'Ace' using ancymidol bulb-dips. *HortScience* 17:336–337.

Marousky, F. J., and S. S. Woltz. 1977. Influence of lime, nitrogen, and phosphorus sources on the availability and relationship of soil fluoride to leaf scorch in *Lilium longiflorum* Thunb. *J. Amer. Soc. Hort. Sci.* 102:799–804.

Mastalerz, J. W. 1965. Bud blasting in *Lilium longiflorum. Proc. Amer. Soc. Hort. Sci.* 87:502–509.

Matsukawa, T., and M. Kashiwagi. 1971. Growth inhibition by mechanical stimulation in horticultural plants. *Abstr. Autumn Mtg. Japanese Soc. Hort. Sci.* pp. 286–287 (in Japanese).

McWhorter, F. P. 1957. Easter lily fungus diseases. *Handbook on bulb growing and forcing.* Northwest Bulb Growers Assn. 196 pp.

Merritt, R. H. 1963. Vegetative and floral development of plants resulting from differential precooling of planted 'Croft' lily bulbs. *Proc. Amer. Soc. Hort. Sci.* 82:517–525.

Miller, R. O. 1985. Lilies. pp. 575–596. In: V. Ball (ed.), *Ball RedBook* Reston Press, Reston, VA.

Miller, R. O., and D. C. Kiplinger. 1966a. Interaction of temperature and time of vernalization on Northwest Easter lilies. *Proc. Amer. Soc. Hort. Sci.* 88:635–645.

Miller, R. O., and D. C. Kiplinger. 1966b. Reversal of vernalization in Northwest Easter lilies. *Proc. Amer. Soc. Hort. Sci.* 88:646–650.

Miller, W. B., and R. W. Langhans. 1985. Growth and productivity of 'Grand Rapids' lettuce in diurnally fluctuating temperature and day/night average temperatures. *J. Amer. Soc. Hort. Sci.* 110:560–565.

Miller, W. B., and R. W. Langhans. 1986. Factors and possible causes of bud abortion in Easter lily. *HortScience* 21:258 (Abstr.).

Miller, W. B., and R. W. Langhans. 1989a. Reduced irradiance affects dry weight partitioning in Easter lily. *J. Amer. Soc. Hort. Sci.* 114:306–309.

Miller, W. B., and R. W. Langhans. 1989b. Carbohydrate changes in Easter lilies during growth in normal and reduced irradiance environments. *J. Amer. Soc. Hort. Sci.* 114:310–315.

Neel, P. L., and R. W. Harris. 1971. Motion-induced inhibition of elongation and induction of dormancy in *Liquidambar. Science* 173:58–59.

Niimi, Y., and M. Oda. 1989. Time of initiation and development of flowerbuds in *Lilium rubellum* Baker. *Scientia Hortic.* 39:341–348.

Oliver, G. W. 1908. The production of Easter lily bulbs in the United States. *U.S. Dept. Agric. Bul.* 120. 24 pp.

Pennell, J., and G. Johnson. 1967. Insects, pp. 119–135. In: D. C. Kiplinger and R. W. Langhans (eds.), *Lilies. The Culture, Diseases, Insects and Economics of Easter Lilies.* Cornell Univ. Press, Ithaca, N.Y.

Peterson, J. C., and L. L. Kramer, 1990. Water quality. pp. 26–27. In: *Tips on Growing Easter Lilies.* The Ohio State Univ., Columbus, Ohio.

Post, K. 1941. Problems in forcing Easter lilies. *Proc. Amer. Soc. Hort. Sci.* 39:415–418.

Prince, T. A., and M. S. Cunningham. 1989. Production

and storage factors influencing quality of potted Easter lilies. *HortScience* 24:992–994.

Prince, T. A., and M. S. Cunningham. 1990. Response of Easter lily bulbs to peat moisture content and the use of peat or of polyethylene lined cases during handling and vernalization. *J. Amer. Soc. Hort. Sci.* 115:68–72.

Prince, T. A., and M. S. Cunningham. 1991. Forcing characteristics of Easter lily bulbs exposed to elevated-ethylene and -carbon dioxide and low-oxygen atmospheres. *J. Amer. Soc. Hort. Sci.* 116:63–67.

Prince, T. A., M. S. Cunningham, and J. S. Peary. 1987. Floral and foliar quality of potted Easter lilies after STS or phenidone application, refrigerated storage, and simulated shipment. *J. Amer. Soc. Hort. Sci.* 112:469–473.

Rhoads, A., J. Troiano, and E. Brennan. 1973. Ethylene gas as a cause of injury to Easter lilies. *Plant Dis. Rptr.* 57:1023–1024.

Roberts, A. N., and F. W. Moeller. 1979. Evidence of genetic tendency to leaf scorch in *Lilium longiflorum* Thunb. 'Ace' inbred lines. *Yrbk. North Amer. Lily Soc.* 32:50–54.

Roberts, A. N, J. R. Stang, Y. T. Wang, W. R. McCorkle, L. R. Riddle, and F. W. Moeller. 1985. Easter lily growth and development. *Oregon State Univ. Agric. Expt. Sta. Tech Bull.* 148. 74 pp.

Roh, S. M. 1982. Propagation of *Lilium longiflorum* Thunb. by leaf cuttings. *HortScience* 17:607–609.

Roh, S. M., and H. F. Wilkins. 1973. Influence of temperature on the development of flower buds from the visible bud stage to anthesis of *Lilium longiflorum* Thunb. cv. Ace. *HortScience* 8:129–130.

Sachs, R. M., A. M. Kofranek, and W. P. Hackett. 1976. Evaluating new pot plant species. *Flor. Rev.* 159(4116):35–36, 80–84.

Senecal, M., B. Dansereau, and R. Paquin. 1989. Fertilization and night temperature effects on growth and carbohydrate status of poinsettia. *Can. J. Plant Sci.* 69:347–349.

Simmonds, J. A., and B. G. Cumming. 1977. Bulb-dip application of growth-regulating chemicals for inhibiting stem elongation of 'Enchantment' and 'Harmony' lilies. *Scientia Hortic.* 6:71–81.

Smith, D. R. 1963. The influence of the environment upon initiation and development in *Lilium longiflorum* (Thunb.). Ph.D. Thesis, Cornell University, Ithaca, N.Y.

Smith, D. R., and R. W. Langhans. 1962a. The influence of day and night temperatures on the growth and flowering of the Easter lily (*Lilium longiflorum* Thunb. var Croft). *Proc. Amer. Soc. Hort. Sci.* 80:593–598.

Smith, D. R., and R. W. Langhans. 1962b. The influence of photoperiod on the growth and flowering of the Easter lily (*Lilium longiflorum* Thunb. var Croft). *Proc. Amer. Soc. Hort. Sci.* 80:599–604.

Staby, G. L., and T. D. Erwin. 1977. The storage of Easter lilies. *Flor. Rev.* 161(4162):38.

Stimart, D. P., and P. D. Ascher. 1978. Tissue culture on bulb scale sections for asexual propagation of *Lilium longiflorum* Thunb. *J. Amer. Soc. Hort. Sci.* 103:182–184.

Stuart, N. W. 1952. Effects of storage temperatures on the forcing responses of Easter lily and bulbous iris. *Rept. 13th Intl. Hortic. Cong.* pp. 515–524.

Stuart, N. W. 1954. Moisture content of packing medium, temperature and duration of storage as factors in forcing lily bulbs. *Proc. Amer. Soc. Hort. Sci.* 63:488–494.

Stuart, N. 1967. Present methods of handling bulbs. In: D. C. Kiplinger and R. W. Langhans (eds.), *Lilies. The Culture, Diseases, Insects and Economics of Easter*

Lilies. Cornell Univ. Press, Ithaca, N.Y.

Stuart, N. W., D. L. Gill, and M. G. Hickman. 1961. Height control of forced Georgia Easter lilies. *Flor. Rev.* 129(3344):13–14, 40–41.

Tammen, J. F., J. R. Oglevee, E. J. Oglevee, and L. Duffy. 1986. A new process for producing pathogen free Easter lilies. *GrowerTalks* July 1986. 50(3):62–66.

Tayama, H. K. 1990. Chemical growth regulators. In: *Tips on Growing Easter Lilies.* The Ohio State Univ., Columbus, Ohio.

Thornton, N.C. 1939. Development of dormancy in lily bulbs. *Contrib. Boyce Thompson Inst.* 10:381–388.

Tincker, M. A. H. 1950. Soil conditions, the growth of lilies and their roots. *Yrbk. North Amer. Lily Soc.* 3:34–47.

Tsujita, M. J., D. P. Murr, and A. G. Johnson. 1978. Influence of phosphorus nutrition and ancymidol on leaf senescence and growth of Easter lily. *Can J. Plant Sci.* 58:287–290.

Tsujita, M. J., D. P. Murr, and G. Johnson. 1979. Leaf senescence of Easter lily as influenced by root/shoot growth, phosphorus nutrition and ancymidol. *Can J. Plant Sci.* 59:757–761.

Tsukushi, R. 1970. The effect of the removal of various flower parts on the senescence and abscission of the perianth of *Lilium longiflorum* cv. Ace. *Ohio Flor. Assn. Bul.* 488:5.

Turgeon, R., and J. A. Webb. 1971. Growth inhibition by mechanical stress. *Science* 174:961–962.

Webster's Third International Dictionary of the English Language. 1981. Merriam-Webster, Springfield, MA.

Weiler, T. C. 1973. Cold and daylength requirements for flowering in a *Lilium longiflorum* Thunb. cultivar. *HortScience* 8:185.

Weiler, T. C., and R. W. Langhans. 1972. Effect of storage temperatures on the flowering and growth of *Lilium longiflorum* (Thunb.) 'Ace'. *J. Amer. Soc. Hort. Sci.* 97:173–175.

Weller, S.C., and P. A. Hammer. 1984. Susceptibility of Easter lily to glyphosate injury. *HortScience* 19:698–699.

White, J. W. 1976. *Lilium* sp. 'Mid Century Hybrids' adapted to pot use with ancymidol. *J. Amer. Soc. Hort. Sci.* 101:126–129.

Wilfret, G. J. 1987. Height retardation of Easter lilies grown in containers. *Proc. Fla. State Hort. Sci.* 100:379–382.

Wilkins, H. F. 1980. Easter lilies. pp. 327–352. In: R. A. Larson (ed.), *Introduction to Floriculture*. Academic Press, New York, N.Y.

Wilkins, H. F., and S. M. Roh. 1977. Even higher flower bud numbers are now possible in Easter lilies by dipping greenhouse temperatures. *Flor. Rev.* 159(4127)33, 76–79.

Wilkins, H. F., W. E. Waters, and R. E. Widmer. 1968. The effect of carbon dioxide, photoperiod and vernalization on flowering of Easter lilies (*Lilium longiflorum* Thunb. 'Ace' and 'Nellie White'). *Proc. Amer. Soc. Hort. Sci.* 96:650–654.

Wilson, E. H. 1925. *The Lilies of Eastern Asia*. Dulau and Co. London.

Wister, J. C. 1930. Lilies. In: *Bulbs for American Gardens*. Stratford Company.

Wulster, G. J., T. J. Gianfagna, and B. B. Clark. 1987. Comparative effects of ancymidol, propiconazol, triadimefon, and Mobay RSW0411 on lily height. *HortScience* 22:601–602.

Zieslin, N., and M. J. Tsujita. 1988. Regulation of stem elongation of lilies by temperature and the effect of gibberellin. *Scientia Hortic.* 37:165–169.